Dictionary of
1000 Russian Proverbs

Dictionary of
1000 Russian Proverbs

with English Equivalents

Peter Mertvago

HIPPOCRENE BOOKS
New York

For information, address:
HIPPOCRENE BOOKS, INC.
171 Madison Avenue
New York, NY 10016

Cataloging-in-Publication Data
Mertvago, Peter.
    Dictionary of 1000 Russian proverbs : with English equivalents /
Peter Mertvago.
        p.   cm.

    ISBN 0-7818-0564-3
    1. Proverbs, Russian. 2. Proverbs, Russian—Translations into
English.   I. Title.
PN6505.S5M386   1997
398.9'9171—dc21   97-39302
                                                                              CIP

INTRODUCTION

This book is a product of the *Comparative Russian-English Dictionary of Russian Proverbs and Sayings* and was prepared to address the specific and immediate needs of readers who wish only to familiarize themselves with the most commonly used Russian proverbs. It therefore further trims down the 1,900 highlighted most important proverbs of the total of 5,543 entries in that previous work to a more tractable minimum core of 1,000 proverbs. Whoever uses the word *minimum* in the context of proverbs has in mind the efforts of paremiologists in the last 25 years to develop *paremiological minima* for various languages, and that in turn—especially in the realm of Russian proverbs—means the pioneering work of the late G.L. Permiakov.[1]

While proverbs had long been a subject of interest to folklorists, linguists and dilettantes, Permiakov was among the first to posit their pragmatic importance in the learning and mastery of foreign languages. Drawn from experience gained in the nascent technique of demographic surveys, he devised an important paremiological *experiment,* as he termed it, to identify the most current proverbs in modern conversational Russian.[2] He distributed a list of 1,494 (1,740 including variants) proverbs, sayings, riddles, apophthegms, and popular dicta among 300 Muscovites and asked them to mark those which were unfamiliar to them and to indicate any of importance which they felt had been omitted. They were also asked to specify their occupation, domicile, level of education and the approximate total number of

---

[1] For a discussion of the present state of this research, see Wolfgang Mieder, "Paremiological Minimum and Cultural Literacy," in *Wise Words: Essays on the Proverb*, edited by W. Mieder (NY: Garland, 1994), pp. 297-316.

[2] G.L. Permiakov, *«Паремиологический эксперимент - материалы для паремиологического минимума. Полторы тысячи русских пословиц, поговорок, загадок, примет и других народных изречений, наиболее распространенных в живой разговорной речи,»* (Москва: Наука, 1971).

proverbs and proverbial expressions they thought they knew—20, 50, 100, 200 or more.

Although the experiment was conducted in Moscow, Permiakov by his own account took care to include in his list expressions which were not only current, but which "we also frequently heard in other parts of the [former] Soviet Union, *inter alia* the Urals, Tula province, Western Siberia, Kazakhstan, as well as among the Russian-speaking population of northern Ukraine."[3] As a result of this survey he was able to conclude that "every adult Russian language speaker (over 20 years of age) knows no fewer than 800 proverbs, proverbial expressions, popular literary quotations and other forms of clichés."[4] Unfortunately, Permiakov died in 1983 before he was able to compile all of his research on this and related subjects in the one volume that he had been planning, so questions persist about the methodology he used for his empirical investigation and the percentages in the replies for the individual entries and answers to the questionnaires.[5] He did however complete his manuscript for a short book of 300 best-known Russian proverbs and proverbial expressions which was published posthumously as *300 общеупотребительных русских пословиц и поговорок (для говорящих на немецком языке)* which, with its introduction, cultural notes and variant entries, may be considered to embody his ideas on the development of paremiological minima, their importance in learning foreign languages, and how they should be presented for cross-cultural comparative purposes.[6]

The present *Dictionary of 1000 Russian Proverbs* differs from Permiakov's so-called minimum in several respects. First, as the title indicates, it has 1000 entries, which brings it more in line with the broader *passive*

---

[3] *ibid.* p.3

[4] *id.* "К вопросу о русском паремиологическом минимуме" in Е.М.Верещагина, ed. *Словари и лингвострановедение (Москва: Русский язык, 1982)*, p.131. English translation by K.J. McKenna, "On the Question of a Russian Paremiological Minimum," *Proverbium* 6 (1989), p.91.

[5] Permiakov's archive is preserved in the Institute of Oriental Studies at the Academy of Sciences of the Russian Federation. Georgii Leonidovich Kapchits compiled much of this material in *Foundations of Structural Paremiology*, ed. I.L. Elevich (Moscow: Nauka), published in 1988, after Permiakov's death and under his name. For a discussion of this work, see Peter Grzybek, "Two Recent Publications in Soviet Structural Paremiology," *Proverbium* 6 (1989), pp.181-186.

[6] A German edition of this book appeared in the same year as *300 allgemeingebräuchliche russische Sprichwörter und sprichwörtliche Redensarten. Ein illustriertes Nachschlagewerk für Deutschsprechende.* (Leipzig: VEB Verlag Enzyklopädie), followed by a Bulgarian edition the year after, for speakers of Bulgarian: *300 общоупотребителни руски пословици и поговорки* (Sofia: Narodna prosveta, 1986).

paremiological minimum that Permiakov identified prior to selecting what can be assumed to be his *active minimum* of 300.[7] In the present work, these 300 texts have been marked with an asterisk (*). In actual fact their number here is not 300 but 246, which arises from the second main difference, and that is that the present *Dictionary* includes only proverbs while Permiakov's work also had sayings and proverbial expressions that could not be classified as proverbs.

It is true that a proper definition of what exactly constitutes a proverb has caused much commentary. One can follow Permiakov and apply a functional *semiotic* designation that proverbs act as signs of situations or of relationships between objects around us in the real world, or one may prefer the structural approach taken by Dundes in analyzing the oppositional characteristics of proverbs.[8] But such elaborate efforts still leave one hungering for a simpler solution and people often feel more comfortable with apt characterizations like those of Cervantes: "short sentences based on long experience," or Lord Russell: "the wisdom of many, the wit of one." This is not surprising since it is in the very nature of the beast—proverbs being the common baggage of humankind—and we are more happy to conclude with scholars like B.J. Whiting that "no definition is really necessary, since all of us know what a proverb is."[9] Be that as it may, the present work lists only Russian proverbs that can grammatically stand alone as complete sentences and therefore does not include phrases and other expressions, for which the reader may be referred to the larger *Comparative Dictionary*.

In providing English equivalents for Russian proverbs, the present *Dictionary* distinguishes between lexical and semiotic equivalents. The former are Russian proverbs that have an exact or nearly exact word-for-word equivalent in English, most likely as a result of derivation from a common stock of proverbs, so that the same proverb may exist in both languages in identical or easily recognizable alternate forms. In such cases the English proverbs are given under the Russian entries in normal type. In those instances

---

[7] *Proverbium* 22 (1973) p.863.

[8] G.L. Permiakov, *From Proverb to Folk Tale. Notes on the General Theory of Cliché.* (Moscow: Nauka, 1979), p.20 and Alan Dundes, "On the Structure of the Proverb," *Proverbium* 25 (1975), pp. 961-973. For a discussion of the structure of the Russian proverb, see also P.Mertvago, *op.cit.*, Introduction, pp.iii-vi, and Appendix 2, pp. 380-389.

[9] "Proverbs and Proverbial Sayings: Introduction." *The Franck C. Brown Collection of N. Carolina Folklore*, vol.1 (Durham, N. Carolina 1952), p.331. For a discussion of this viewpoint see Dundes, *op.cit.*. pp.961. 971 and note 8.

however where no lexically-equivalent proverb occurs in English, the *Dictionary* lists *in italic type* the English proverbs that could be thought of as semiotic equivalents—*i.e.,* that could be used in similar contexts or circumstances. In these entries, literal translations of the original Russian proverbs are given within square brackets [ ]. Similarly, any lexical departure from the Russian in an identical English proverb is identified by means of brackets [denoting literal translation] and italics, *equivalent English proverb.*

To make the *Dictionary* more user-friendly, the strict alphabetical arrangement of Russian entries by first word that was used in the larger *Comparative Dictionary* has been abandoned in favor of an alphabetical listing by key words, which is the preferred format today for dictionaries of this type. What is meant by *key word* for this purpose is the sequentially first noun most closely associated with the meaning of the proverb and/or having a greater linguistic range or frequency. For proverbs without nouns, key words may be verbs, adjectives or adverbs identified on the basis of the same considerations. To make the *Dictionary* useful from English into Russian and to facilitate finding proverbs, an English key word index has been provided. Throughout the *Dictionary*, alternate forms of proverbs or alternate words or phrases used in the same proverb have been placed within parentheses in the entry that represents the most common form of the proverb. A separate Russian key word index has been given at the end of the book to facilitate finding entries on the basis of the key words used in such alternate forms. Cross references have been provided for similar proverbs, and these are indicated by the symbol *Cf.*

The author wishes to express special thanks to Professor Wolfgang Mieder of the University of Vermont for making available to him certain indispensable texts of Permiakov's works, and to his own wife Ludmila for her help in the laborious task of preparing the manuscript for publication.

Peter Mertvago

А

Ад	1	Ад вымощен благими намерениями. (Добрыми намерениями дорога в ад устлана.) Hell is paved with good intentions.
	2	По привычке и в аду живут. (Привыкнешь, и в аде живешь.) [One can even get used to living in Hell.] *One can get used to everything, even hanging.*
Алмаз	3	Алмаз алмазом гранится (решится). Diamond cut diamond.
Алтын	4	Пожалеть алтына, потерять полтина. Penny wise and pound foolish.
Ананья	5	В людях Ананья (Илья) (ангел), а дома каналья (свинья) (черт). A saint [Ananya (Ilya)] abroad and a devil [(pig)] at home. An angel on the street, a devil at home.
	6	Каков Ананья, такова у него Маланья. Every *Jack* [Ananya] has his *Jill* [Melania].

Аннушка	7	Хороша дочь Аннушка коли хвалит мать да бабушка. [Annie's a fine girl according to her mother or grandmother.] *No mother has a homely child.* **Cf.** 473
Аппетит	8*	Аппетит приходит во время еды. Appetite comes with eating.
Апрель	9	Апрель с водой, а май с травой. April showers bring May flowers.
Аукнуться	10*	Как аукнется, так и откликнется. (Каков привет, таков и ответ.) As you salute, you will be saluted. *Such answer as a man gives, such will he get.*

Б

Баба   11   Две бабы - базар, три - ярмарка.
(Гусь да баба - торг, два гуся, две бабы - ярмарка.)
Three women make a market.
Three women and a goose make a market.

12   Не было у бабы хлопот (горя), купила порося.
[The woman had no problems (sorrows) so she bought some pigs.]
We carry our greatest enemies within us.
Nothing's so bad that it couldn't have been worse.

Бабушка   13   Бабушка (старуха) надвое сказала (гадала).
[The grandmother (old lady) said (foretold) it ambiguously.]
We shall see what we shall see.

Барип   14   Бары (паны) дерутся а у холопов чубы болят.
The humble suffer from the folly of the great.
The pleasures of the mighty are the tears of the poor. *Cf.* 14, 404

Беда   15   Беда беду накликает (родит).
Trouble breeds trouble.

16*   Беда не приходит одна.
(Придет беда, отворяй ворота.)
Misfortunes never come alone (singly). *Cf.* 186

17 Беда приходит пудами а уходит золотниками.
(Болезнь к нам верхом, а от нас пешком.)
(Зло к нам летит а от нас ползет.)
Mischief comes by the pound and goes away by the ounce.
Diseases come on horseback but depart on foot.
Misfortunes come on wings and depart on foot.
Ill comes in ells and goes out by inches.

18 Беду не ждут (горе не ищут) - она сама приходит.
Sorrow comes unsent for.

19 Без беды и добра не бывает.
(Горе и радость ходят вместе.)
(Доход не живет без хлопот.)
No pains, no gains.
No cross, no crown.
The way to bliss lies not on beds of down. **Cf.** 696, 861, 946

20 Никогда не надо чужой беде смеяться.
Never rejoice about your neighbor's misfortunes.

21* Семь бед, один ответ.
[Seven wrongs - one punishment.]
As well be hanged for a sheep as for a lamb.
Over shoes, over boots.

22 Чужая беда людям смех.
Everything is funny as long as it happens to someone else.

Бедность	23*	Бедность не грех (порок) (стыд). Poverty is no sin (shame).
Бедный	24	Бедному жениться - ночь коротка. [The night's too short to warrant marrying poor.] *Who marries for love without money has good nights and sorry days.*
	25	На бедного везде капнет. (Бедному везде бедно.) [It always rains on the poor.] *The poor suffer all the wrong.* *The poor man is aye put to the worst. Cf. 467*
Безделье	26	Безделье - мать пороков. Idleness is the mother (root) of all evil (sin) (vice).
Безумный	27	Безумный и разумных ума лишает. [A fool strips even the wise of reason.] *One fool makes many.*
Берег	28	Хорошо тому смеяться, кто на сухом берегу. Nothing is more delightful than to look upon danger from a place of safety.
Бесстыжий	29	Бесстыжему город велик. [The city is great for the shameless.] *For he who is without shame, all the world is his.*

Бесчестье	30	Бесчестье хуже смерти. Better death than dishonor. *Cf.* 783
Битый	31	Битого, пролитого да прожитого не воротишь. [What's broken, spilt, or done can ne'er be undone.] *It is no use crying over spilt milk. Cf.* 141, 887
	32*	За одного битого (ученого) двух небитых (неученых) (неучей) дают. [One beaten (learned) man is worth two who are unscathed (ignorant).] *A thimbleful of experience is worth a tubful of knowledge.* *A thorn of experience is worth a wilderness of advice.*
Благо- деяние	33	Благодеяние свершить никогда пе поздно. It's never too late to do good.
Ближе	34	Всяк (всякий) сам себе ближе (дороже). Every man is nearest himself. *Cf.* 716, 890
Блин	35*	Первый блин (всегда) комом. [The first *blin* (pancake) always turns out lumpy.] *If at first you don't succeed, try again.*

Блоха	36	Осердясь на блохи (вши) да и шубу (одеяло) в печь. [Burn one's fur (blanket) to get rid of the fleas (lice).] *Burn one's house to get rid of the mice.*
Бог	37*	Береженого (и) Бог бережет. (Кто работает, тому Бог помогает.) God (heaven) helps them that help themselves.
	38	Бог даст день, даст и пищу. (Дал Бог роток, даст и хлеб.) (Родится роток - родится и кусок.) God never sends mouth but he sends meat.
	39	Бог долго ждет, да больно бьет. God comes with leaden feet but strikes with iron hands.
	40	Бог по силе крест налагает. God shapes the back for the burden
	41*	Бог-то Бог, да и сам не будь плох. (Богу молись, а сам трудись.) *Pray to God, but keep hammering (but hammer away).* *Trust in God and do something.* **Cf.** 47

42* Бог троицу любит.
(Без тройцы дом не строится.)
(Трою числом лучше.)
[God loves threes.]
(All) good things come in threes.
All things thrive at thrice.
Number three is always fortunate.

43 Все под Богом ходим.
All men are mortal.

44 Где Бог себе строит церковь, там дьявол часовню.
Where God has his church, the devil will have his chapel. *Cf.* 952

45 Кого хочет Бог наказать, у того отнимает разум.
When God will punish, he will first take away the understanding.

46 Лучше «слава Богу» нежели «дай Бог.»
[Better to say "Thank God" than "God willing."]
Better to have than to wish.

47* На Бога надейся (положись) (уповай), а сам не плошай.
[Trust in God, but don't be remiss.]
Work as if everything depended on you, pray as if everything depended on God. *Cf.* 41

Богатый	48	Богатому богатство и вяжется. The rich get richer. *Cf.* 235

49 Богатому везде дом.
(Богатому завсе праздник.)
[The rich man is at home everywhere (always on holiday).]
Money makes a man free (recommends a man) everywhere.
The rich man has the world by the tail.

50 Богаты не будем а сыты будем.
[We won't be rich but we'll have enough to eat.]
He is rich enough who lacks not bread.
Enough is great riches.

51 Богатый всегда в страхе.
[The rich man is always in fear.]
Much coin, much care. *Cf.* 233

52 Богатый как хочет, а бедный как может.
Rich men may have what they will poor men what they can.

53 У богатого груз в корабле, у бедного хлеб на уме.
Poor men seek meat for their stomachs, rich men stomachs for their meat.

	54	У богатого телята, у бедного ребята. A rich man for dogs and a poor man for babies. The rich get richer and the poor have children.
	55*	Чем богаты, тем и рады. (Тот богат кто своим счастьем доволен.) He is not rich that possesses much, but he that is content with what he has.
Богач	56	Скупой богач беднее нищего. A rich miser is poorer than a poor man.
Болезнь	57	Легко здоровому болезнь рассуждать. The healthful man can give counsel to the sick.
Болеть	58*	У кого что болит (что кого веселит), тот о том и говорит. [Everyone talks about what pains (pleases) them.] *Have a bee in one's bonnet.* *Everyone speaks of his own interest.*
Большой	59	Что говорит большой, слышит и малый. [What the adult says, the youngster hears.] *Little pitchers have long ears.*
Борозда	60	Стар (старый конь) (старая кобыла) борозды не испортит. An old ox makes a straight furrow.

Бочка	61	Бочка пахнет тем что в ней раньше было. The cask savors of the first fill.
	62	В пустой бочке звону больше. (Пустой колос голову кверху носит.) Empty barrels (vessels) make the greatest noise (sound). *A humble bee in a cow turd thinks himself king.*
Брань	63	Брань на вороту не виснет. [Insults won't stick to your collar.] *Words may pass but blows fall heavy. Cf.* 190, 994
Брат	64	Без брата проживу, а без соседа не проживу. *We can live without our friends* [brother] *but not our neighbors.*
Бремя	65	Легко мнится бремя (ноша) на чужой спине (чужом плече). The burden is light on the shoulders of another.
Брод	66*	Не зная (спросясь) броду, не суйся в воду. Never wade in unknown waters. *Look before you leap.*
Брюхо	67	Брюхо сыто да глаза голодны. The eye is bigger than the belly.
	68	Сытое брюхо к учению глухо (туго). A belly full of gluttony will never study willingly.

	69	У брюха нет ушей. The belly wants ears.
Булат	70	Булат железо и кисель режет. [The same sword can cut both steel and jelly.] *The same knife cuts bread and fingers.*
Бумага	71*	Бумага все терпит (Бумага без души - что угодно пиши). Paper is patient - you can put anything on it. *Paper won't blush.*
Бык	72	Всякий бык был теленком. [Every bull was once a lamb.] *Every oak has been an acorn.*
Быть	73*	Чему быть, того (тому) не миновать. What will be, will (shall) be.
	74	Что было, то сплыло (то былью поросло). What's done is done. Let bygones be bygones. *Cf.* 141, 837

В

Ванна	75	Выплеснуть из ванны вместе с водой и ребенка. Throw the baby out with the bath water.
Ваня	76	Чему Ваня не научился, того Иван не выучит. What Johnny will not teach himself, Johnny will never know.
Везде	77	Кто везде, тот нигде. [Who is everywhere is nowhere.] *He who begins many things finishes but few.*
Век	78*	Век живи, век учись (+ а дураком помрешь). Live and learn. (+ and die a fool).
	79	Не равны (бывают) веки, не равны и человеки. Times change and (people change their ideas) (we) with them.
Веревка	80*	Сколько веревку не вить, а концу быть. [Regardless of how long you may make a rope, it will always have an end.] *Everything has an end.* *At length the fox is brought to the furrier.*

Весть	81	Хороши вести что нечего ести. No news is good news.
	82	Худые вести не лежат на месте. (Худая молва на крыльях летит.) Bad news travels fast.
Ветер	83	Кто посеет ветер, пожнет бурю. Sow the wind and reap the whirlwind.
	84	Против ветра не подуешь. Puff not against the wind.
Вещь	85	Береженая вещь два века живет. [Something well cared for lasts two centuries.] *An old cart well used may outlast a new one abused.* **Cf.** 246
	86	Вещь хороша когда новая, а друг - старый. New things are the best things, but old friends are the best friends. **Cf.** 265
Видеть	87	Лучше видеть нежели слышать. (Виденное лучше сказанного.) (Лучше один раз увидеть чем сто раз услышать.) Seeing is believing. Better seen than heard. *One eyewitness is better than two hear-so's (ten hearsays).*

	88	Не видит, так и не бредит. Unseen, unrued.
	89	Реже видишь, милее будешь. Absence makes the heart grow fonder. *Cf.* 195
Визг	90	Визгу много а шерсти нет. Great cry and little wool.
Вина	91	Всякая вина виновата. The faulty stands on his guard. *The smaller the wrong, the greater the guilt.*
Вино	92	Вино входит, ум выходит. When wine is in, wit is out.
	93	Доброе вино не нуждается в этикетке. Good wine needs no bush.
	94	Не вино винит, но пьянство. (Невинно вино, виновато пьянство.) Intoxication is not the wine's fault but man's.
	95	Поздно беречь вино когда бочка пуста. Better spare at brim than at bottom. When the wine is run out, you stop the leak.
Виноватый	96	В миру виноватого нет. The fault is always someone else's

	97	Где все виноваты, там никто не виноват. When everyone is wrong, everyone is right.
	98	Кто посмирней, тот и виноват. Secret guilt by silence is betrayed.
Вкус	99*	На вкус (на любовь), на цвет товарища (спора) (образца) нет. (О вкусах не спорят.) There is no accounting (disputing) for (about) tastes. *Cf.* 639
Вместе	100*	Вместе тесно, а врозь скучно. [Too crowded together, to dull apart.] *Can't live with each other, can't live without each other.* *Those we love, we can hate.* *The quarrels of lovers is the renewal of love.*
Вода	101	Воду варить (в ступе толочь), вода и будет. (Как пустую воду ни вари, а навару не дождешься.) [Boil (beat) water and it's still water (you won't get grease on the ssurface).] *Whether you boil snow or pound it, you can have but water of it.*
	102	Пролив (пролитую) воду, не поймаешь (соберешь). Spilled water cannot be gathered up.

103   Стоячая вода плеснеет.
Standing pools gather filth.

104   Тихие воды глубоки.
Still waters run deep. *Cf.* 298

105   Тяжело против воды плыть.
It is ill (evil) striving against the stream.
No striving against the stream. *Cf.* 708

Воз   106*   Что с возу упало, то (давно) пропало.
[What has fallen off the cart is lost forever.]
For a lost thing, care not.

Волвянка   107   Первая волвянка в кузов.
[The first mushroom goes in the basket.]
The first dish pleases all.

Волга   108   В ложке Волги не переедешь.
(Челном море/океана не переехать.)
It is hard to sail over the sea in an egg-shell.

Волк   109   Волк волка не съест.
[Wolf does not eat wolf.]
Dog does not eat dog. Cf. 135, 804

110   Волк кается, а за овцу хватается.
[A wolf bewails the sheep, then eats it.]
*Carrion crows bewail the dead
sheep, then eat them. Cf.* 121

111*   Волка (треску) бояться - (так) в лес не ходить.
He that fears leaves [wolves] *must not
go into the wood.*

112   Волка бояться и от белки бежать.
[He who fears wolves also runs from squirrels.]
When a serpent has bitten, a lizard alarms.

113   Волком родился (родясь) - лисой (лисицей) не бывать.
[What is born a wolf cannot become a fox.]
*He who is born round cannot die square. **Cf.** 626*

114*   И волки сыты и овцы целы.
(Коза сыта а капуста цела.)
[The wolves (goat) are (is) sated and the sheep are safe (the cabbage is intact).]
Have both the egg and the hen.
Neither pot broken nor water spilt.

115   Ловит волк, да ловят и волка.
[The wolf hunts and is himself hunted.]
Long runs the fox but at last is caught.
The smartest fox is caught at last.

116*   Меж(ду) (с) волками быть (жить) - волком и выть (по волчьи выть).
Who keeps company with the wolf, will learn to howl.

117   На волке волчья и шерсть.
[The wolf has a wolf's hide.]
Whoever is a wolf behaves as a wolf.

118*   О волке речь, а он навстречь.
(На ловца и зверь бежит.)
[The prey comes to the hunter.]
Speak of the devil [wolf] and he is sure to appear.
The ball comes to the player.

119   Один волк гоняет овец полк.
It never troubles the wolf how many the sheep may be.

120   От волка (дыма) бежал, да (и) на медведя напал (в огонь упал).
(От беды/горя бежал, да в пропасть/беду попал.)
Shunning the smoke, they fall into the fire.
Escaped the thunder and fell into the lightning.
Out of the frying pan and into the fire. **Cf.** 573

121   Пожалел волк кобылу, оставил хвост да гриву.
[The wolf pitied the mare so he left its tail and mane.]
Crows weep for the dead lamb and then devour him. **Cf.** 110

122*   Сколько (как) волка ни корми, а он все к лесу глядит.
(Волк линяет, но нрав не меняет.)
The wolf may lose his coat (teeth), but never his nature.

Воля	123	Вольному воля, спасенному рай. [Freedom for the free and heaven for the saved.] *It's a free country. To each his own.* *As the fool thinks, so the bell clinks.*
Вор	124	Большой вор малого воришку вешает. Great thieves hang little ones.
	125	Вор думает что все на свете воры. The thief thinks that everyone else is a thief.
	126	Вора миловать - доброго погубить. *Pardoning the bad* [thief] *is injuring the good.*
	127	Где плохо лежит, туда вор глядит. The hole calls the thief. Opportunity makes the thief.
	128	Два вора дерутся - честному польза. When thieves fall out, honest men come to their own.
	129	Кто вору потакает, тот сам вор. The receiver is as bad as a thief.
	130*	На воре (тате) шапка горит. (Виноватому все кажется что про него говорят.) He that commits a fault thinks everyonepeaks of it. *A guilty conscience needs no accuser.*

131* Не пойман - не вор (тать).
[No man is a thief until he's caught.]
A man is innocent until proven guilty.

132 У вора ремесло на лбу не написано.
Nobody calls himself a rogue.

133 Худой вор который в своей деревне ворует.
[It is a wicked thief who steals in his own village.]
The fox (wolf) preys furthest from his home (den).
*It is an ill bird that fouls his own nest. **Cf.** 682*

Воробей 134 Старого воробья на мякине не обманешь.
You cannot catch old birds with chaff.

Ворона 135 Ворон ворону глаза не выклюет.
Crows will not pick out crows' eyes. ***Cf.*** 109, 804

136 Ворона за море летала, да вороной и вернулась (а умнее не стала).
[The crow flew over the sea but returned still a crow (none the smarter).
If an ass goes a-traveling, he'll not come home a horse.

	137	Вороне соколом не бывать.
		(Из совы сокол не будет.)
		(Сова хоть бы под небеса летала, а все соколом не будет.)
		A carrion kite [crow] *will never make a good hawk* [falcon].
		A buzzard never makes a good hawk.
	138	Вороны везде черные.
		Crows are black the world over.
	139*	Пуганая ворона (и) куста боится.
		Birds once snared fear all bushes. *Cf.* 396, 502
	140	Старый ворон даром не каркнет.
		An old dog barks not in vain.
Воротить	141	Пролитого да прожитого не воротишь.
		(Что ушло/окоротишь, того не воротишь.)
		What's done cannot be undone.
		Things past cannot be recalled. **Cf.** 31, 74
Воскресение	142	В воскресение веселье, в понедельник похмелье.
		[Part Sunday, hangover Monday.]
		Drunken days have all their tomorrows.

Враг	143	Врагу места много. [Give an enemy much room.] *For a flying enemy, make a golden bridge.*
	144	Лучшее - враг хорошего. Best is the enemy of the good.
	145	Не бойся врага умного, бойся друга глупого. A rash friend is worse than a foe. A wise enemy is better than a foolish friend.
Время	146	В тихое время, всяк может править. Anyone can be a sailor (pilot) on a calm sea.
	147	(Потерянного) времени не (по)воротишь. Time lost (past) cannot be recalled.
	148	Время все излечивает (изнуряет). (Всякое горе с временем забывается.) Time cures all things.
	149	Время всему научит. (Время покажет.) Time reveals (discloses) all things. Time will tell.
	150	Время летит. Time flies.
	151	Время - лучший лекарь (врач) (советчик). Time is the best healer.

152   Время не ждет.
Time waits for no man.

153*   Всему свое время (свой век) (свой черед).
(Всякой вещи - свое время.)
Everything has its time (in turn).

154   Другие времена, другие нравы.
Other times, other manners.

Выиграть   155   Стоит выиграть чтоб не бояться проиграть.
[One must win in order not to fear losing.]
Still he fishes that catches one.

Г

Галка	156	Бей галку (сороку) и ворону, добьешься и до ясного сокола (белого лебедя). [Shoot a daw (magpie) and a crow, and soon you'll hit a falcon (white swan).] *Use the little to get to the big.* **Cf.** 337
Гвоздь	157	На одном гвозде всего не повесишь. Do not hang everything on one nail.
Глаз	158	Видишь глаз чужой, да не видишь свой. The eye that sees all things else sees not itself.
	159	Глаз (око) видит, да зуб неймет. [The eye can see but the tooth cannot bite.] *There's many a slip 'twixt the cup and the lip.*
	160	Глаза - зеркало души. The eye is the mirror (window) of the soul.
	161*	С глаз долой - из сердца вон. (Вон/далеко из глаз/очей, вон/далеко из сердца.) Far from eye, far from heart. Out of sight, out of mind.

Глупый	162	Глупый погрешит один, а умный соблазнит многих. The fool errs alone whereas the wise man corrupts many.
	163	Из ученого глуп бывает. [A scholar may sometimes be a fool.] *Folly and learning often dwell together.*
	164	Один глупый бросит (кинет) камень в воду, а сто умных не вынут. A fool may throw into a well a stone which a hundred wise men cannot pull out.
	165	Умного иногда и глупый на разум наставит. A fool may give a wise man counsel.
Глухой	166	Глухому две обедни не поют (служат). [Mass is not repeated for the deaf.] *Whistle (sing) psalms to the taffrail (a dead horse).*
Гнев	167	Гнев - недолгое безумие. Anger is a short madness.
Говорить	168	Кто говорит что хочет, услышит чего не хочет. He who says what he likes, shall hear what he does not like.

169* Не говори гоп, пока не перепрыгнешь (перескочишь).
[Don't cry "hurrah" until after you have jumped.]
Do not halloo till you're out of the wood.

170 Не говори как что знать.
Do not reveal your sources.

171 Не говори что не могу, говори что не хочу.
I can't means I won't.

Голова 172* Выше головы (носа) не прыгнешь (поднимешь).
[You cannot jump (raise your nose) higher than your head.]
A man can do no more than he can. **Cf.** 217, 446

173* Дурная голова ногам покою не дает.
(За дурной головой и ногам непокой.)
What your head forgets, your heels must remember.
What you haven't got in your head, you have in your heels.

174 Своя голова болит, чужой не лечат.
[When your own head aches, do not treat another's.]
Physician, heal thyself.

175 Сколько голов, столько умов.
So many men (heads), so many minds (wits).

176*   Снявши голову по волосам не плачут.
(Перед смертью не надышишься.)
[Cry not for the hair when the head is off (too late to catch your breath when its time to die).]
It's too late to stoop when the head is off.

Голод   177   Голод и волка из лесу гонит.
(Нужда и голод погоняет на холод.)
Hunger drives the wolf out of the woods.

178   Голод - лучший повар (соус).
Hunger is the best chef (sauce).

Голубь   179   Жаренные голуби сами в рот не влетят.
(Хлеб за брюхом не ходит.)
Roasted ducks don't fly into your mouth. *Cf.* 1000

Голь   180   Голь на выдумки хитра.
[Need is cunning at inventiveness.]
Necessity is the mother of invention.

Гора   181*   Гора с горой не сходится, а человек с человеком сойдется (свидится).
Friends may meet, but mountains never greet.

182   Дулась гора родами, а родила мышь.
The mountains have brought forth a mouse.

183* Если гора не идет к Магомету, Магомет идет к горе.
(Не идет место к голове, но голова к месту.)
If the mountain will not come to Mahomet, Mahomet must go to the mountain.

184 Ты на гору, а черт за ногу.
[You go up the hill and the devil grabs your foot.]
Life is just one damned thing after another.
Life is a bitch.

Горбатый 185* Горбатого исправит могила (+ а упрямого - дубина).
[The grave will straighten the hunchback (+ and the rod the obdurate).]
That which is crooked cannot be made straight.
The crooked log (rod) is not to be straightened.

Горе 186 Одно горе идет по пятам другого.
Ill comes often on the back of worse. *Cf.* 16

Горшок 187 Горшку с котлом не биться.
(Горшок чугуну не товарищ.)
The earthen pot must keep clear of the brass kettle.

188 Горшок котлу смеется (завидует), а оба черны.
(Осудил горшок чугунку, а сам весь в саже.)
The pot calls the kettle black.

189   На всякий горшок найдется покрышка.
Every pot has its cover.

190   Назови (называй) хоть горшком, только в печку не ставь (сажай).
[Call me a pot but put me not on the stove.]
Sticks and stones may break my bones but names will never hurt me.
Cf. 63, 994

191*   Не боги горшки обжигают.
[It's not the gods who fire pots.]
Whatever man has done, man can do.

Горький   192   Не вкусив (вкусить) горького, не едать (видать) сладкого.
Suffering is bitter but its fruits are sweet.

Господин   193   Двум господам не служат.
No man can serve two masters.

Гость   194*   В гостях хорошо, а дома лучше.
[It's nice to be a guest, but home is best.]
East or west, home is best.

195   Хорош гость когда редко ходит.
(Редкое свидание, приятный гость.)
(Частые гости наскучат.)
A constant guest is never welcome.
Short visits make long friends. *Cf.* 89

Грех	196	В чем грех, в том и спасение. Seek your salve where you get your sore
	197	Тайный грех в половину прощен. Sin that is hidden is half forgiven.
Гриб	198	Не поклонясь грибу до земли, не поднять его в кузов. [Without stooping down for the mushroom, you cannot put it in your basket.] *He that would have the fruit must climb the tree.*
Грива	199	Не удержался за гриву, за хвост не удержаться. [He who has let slip the mane will not grip the tail.] *He who would not when he could, is not able when he would.*
Гроза	200	Где гроза тут и ведро. (После грозы/ненастья и ведро будет.) After a storm comes the calm. After black clouds, clear weather.
Грозить	201	Кто много грозит, тот мало вредит. [He that threatens much, harms little.] *Great barkers are no biters.* **Cf.** 784, 801

Гром	202	Гром не гранит - мужик не перекрестится. When it thunders, the thief becomes honest [crosses himself]. *Danger past, God is forgotten. **Cf.** 879*
Грош	203	Легко на чужие гроши ехать. [It is easy to ride at another's cost.] *It is easy to cry Yule at other men's cost.*
	204*	Не было ни гроша, да (и) вдруг алтын. [From penniless to silver.] *From rags to riches.* *It never rains but it pours.*
Груздь	205*	Назвался груздем (грибом), полезай в кузов. [If you call yourself a mushroom, get in the basket.] *In for a penny, in for a pound.* *Don't say go but gaw.*
Гуж	206*	Взялся (взявши) за гуж, не говори что не дюж. [Once you've taken the harness, don't say you're not up to it.] *Never make a promise if you don't intend to keep it.*

Д

Давать	207*	Дают - бери, бьют - беги. [Take when given but run rather than fight.] *Be the first at a feast and the last at a fight.*
	208	Дважды дает кто скоро дает. He gives twice who gives quickly.
	209	Кому много дано, с того много и спросится. [To whom much is given, much is asked of.] *Higher duties mean greater responsibilities.*
Дальше	210	Отскочил чтобы дальше прыгнуть. We must recoil a little to the end we may leap the better.
Дар	211	Всяк дар в строку. [Every gift is recorded.] *Benefits bind.*
Даром	212	Даром никто ничего не выйграет. (Барышу наклад большой брат.) Nothing in this life is free. ([Expense is profit's elder brother.]) *Nothing ventured, nothing gained.*
Двое	213	Двое (два) одному рать. Two to one is odds.

Деготь	214*	Ложка дегтю портит бочку меда. [A spoonful of tar will mar a keg of honey.] *A fly in the ointment.* *One drop of poison infects the whole tun of wine.*
Делаться	215	Что ни делается, все к лучшему. Whatever happens is for the best.
Дело	216	Больше верь делам нежели словам. Judge a man by his deeds, not by his words.
	217*	Всех дел не переделаешь. [You can't do everything.] *Doing everything is doing nothing.* *A man can do no more than he can.* **Cf.** 172
	218	Дело делу учит. In doing we learn.
	219*	Дело мастера боится. [Work fears a master.] *Work fears a resolute man.*
	220*	Делу время - а потехе (отдыху) час. [There is time for work but only an hour for rest (leisure).] *Business before pleasure.*

221   Доброе дело само себя хвалит.
The good deed will praise itself.

222*   (За)кончил дело - гуляй смело.
[When the job's done, step boldly.]
Work well-done makes pleasure more fun.

223   Не начинай дело выше меры.
[Do not begin over your head.]
Never bite off more than you can chew. *Cf.* 527,
537

224   После дела за советом не ходят.
When a thing is done, advice comes too late.

225   Хорошее дело два века живет.
A good deed is never lost.

Демид   226   Всякий Демид себе норовит.
Every man draws water to his own mill.
A man is a lion in his own cause.

День   227   В один день по две радости не живет.
(Дважды лето не бывает.)
You can't have two *forenoons* [joys] in the same
day.
Christmas [summer] comes but once a year. *Cf.*
496

228   День придет и заботу принесет.
No day passes without some grief

229   День сегодняшний - ученик вчерашнего.
Today is the scholar of yesterday.
Today is yesterday's pupil.

230   День хвалится вечером.
(Вечер покажет каков был день.)
Praise a fair day at night.
The evening praises (crowns) the day.

231   Нет такого дня за которым бы ночи не было.
With every day comes night. *Cf.* 549

Деньги   232   Без денег на базар не ходят.
[You don't go moneyless to market.]
A moneyless man goes fast through market.

233   Без денег сон крепче.
[Sleep is sounder without money.]
Little goods, little cares. *Cf.* 51

234   Береги денежку про черный день.
Lay up (*keep something*) for a *rainy* [dark] day.

235 Деньга деньгу достает (деньги идут к деньгам).
Money begets (breeds) (draws) (gets) money. *Cf.* 48

236 Деньгам все повинуется.
(Деньги всему голова.)
All things are obedient to money.
Money is the only monarch.

237 Деньги найдут друга.
Rich folk have many friends.

238 Деньги не пахнут.
Money has no smell.

239* Деньги (денежки) счет любят.
[Money loves accounts.]
Always keep exact accounts.

240* Не в деньгах счастье.
Money can't buy happiness.

241 По деньгам и товар.
You get what you pay for.

242 У денег глаз нет (нету глаз).
Money is blind.

Деревня	243	Хороша деревня, да слава худа.

[It's a good village but it has a bad name.]

Give a dog a bad name and hang him.

The devil is not so black as he is painted. **Cf.** 969

Дерево 244 Дерево с одного разу не валится.

(С одного удара дуба не свалишь.)

An oak is not felled by one stroke.

245* Из-за деревьев не видно леса.

Not to see the forest for the trees.

246 Старое дерево скрипит да стоит, а молодое да валится.

(Скрипучее дерево два века стоит.)

[An old tree screeches but stands while the young one falls.

(The old tree stands two centuries.)]

An old cart well used may outlast a new one abused.

A creaking door (gate) hangs long on its hinges.
Cf. 85

247 Смотри дерево по плодам, а человека по делам.

Judge a tree by its fruit.

Judge a man by his deeds, not by his words.

Дети	248	Малые дети малая печаль, большие дети - большая печаль. (Детки маленьки - поесть не дадут, детки велики - пожить не дадут.) (С малыми детками горе, а с большими - вдвое.) Little children, little troubles; big children, big troubles.
	249	Хорошие дети - отцу и матери утешение. Happy is he who is happy in his children.
Дешево	250	Где дешево там и дорого. (Дешевое наводит на дорогое.) Good cheap is dear.
Дитя	251*	Чем бы дитя не тешилось, лишь бы не плакало. [Anything, so long as the child keeps still.] *Anything for a quiet life (for a little peace and quiet).*
Добро	252	От добра добра не ищут. Leave (let) well (enough) alone.
Дождь	253	Дождь падает на злых и добрых. Rain falls alike on the just and unjust.
	254	Мокрый дождя не боится. [A wet man fears no rain.] *Those that have wet their feet care not how deep they wade.*

Долг	255	В долг брать легко, а платит тяжело. A good borrower is a lazy payer.
	256	В долг давать - дружбу терять. (Друга не теряй - взаймы не давай.) Lend your money and lose your friend.
	257*	Долг платежом красен. [A debt's beauty is in the payment.] *One good (ill) turn deserves another.* *Cf.* 906
	258	Долги помнет не тот кто берет, а кто дает. (Ссуды пишут на железной доске, а долги на песке.) Creditors have better memories than debtors.
Дом	259	Дома (хозяину) и стены помогают. At home everything is easy.
Дорога	260	Ближнюю дорогу вдалеке не ищут. Don't go round the world for a shortcut.
	261	На битой (торной) дороге трава не растет. (Где ногой ступить - трава не растет.) Grass doesn't grow on a busy street (highway). You can't grow grass on a beaten track.

Драка	262*	После драки кулаками не машут. (Много храбрых после рати.) [When the fight's over, don't wave your fists. (Many are brave after the battle.)] *When the war is over, then comes help.* *When the ox is down, many are the butchers.* **Cf.** 841
Дрова	263	Дрова хоть и кривы, да прямо горят. (И из кривой трубы дым прямо поднимается.) Crooked logs make straight fires. [(Smoke rises straight even from a bent chimney.)]
Друг	264	Для друга (к милому) и семь верст не околица. For a good friend, *the journey is never too long* [even seven miles is not out of the way].
	265	Друг лучше старый, а платье новое. New things are the best things, but old friends are best friends. **Cf.** 86
	266	Друзей-то много, да друга нет. He that has friends has no friend. He who has many friends has no friends.
	267*	Друзья (друг) познаются (познается) в беде (несчастье). (Друг в нужде - истинный друг.) (Без беды друга не узнаешь.)

A friend is best found in adversity.
A friend in need is a friend indeed.
A friend is never known until needed.

268   Легко друзей найти, да трудно сохранить.
A friend is not so soon gotten as lost.

269   Нет друга - так ищи, а есть - так береги.
Be slow in choosing a friend, but slower in changing him.

270   Новых друзей наживай, а старых не забывай.
Make new friends but keep the old.

271   Осуждая друга, посмотри за собою.
Judge well yourself before you criticize.

272   Ради милого дружка и сережка из ушка.
Anything [even the earing from my ear] for a friend.

273   Свой своему по неволе друг (брат).
(Кровь водой не бывает.)
[One naturally prefers one's own kin(d).]
You may choose your friends, your family is thrust upon you.
An ass to an ass is beautiful.
(Blood is thicker than water.)

274*   Скажи мне кто твой (с кем ты) друг, а я
        скажу кто ты (таков).
        Tell me who your friends are and I'll tell you who
        you are. *Cf.* 627

275*   Старый друг лучше новых двух.
        One old friend is better than two new ones.

Дружба   276*   Дружба дружбой, а служба службой.
        (Хлеб-соль вместе, а табачок врозь.)
        [Friendship is one thing and tobacco (business) is
        another.
        (Don't mix friendship with tobacco.)]
        *Brotherly love for brotherly love, but cheese for
        money.*
        Don't mix business with pleasure.

Дурак   277   Без дураков скучно.
        More fools, more fun.

278   В роде дураков старшего нет.
        [In the family of fools there is no elder.]
        The family of fools is very old.

279   Временем и дурак правду скажет (умно
        говорит).
        A fool may sometimes tell the truth (speak to the
        purpose.)

280   Дурак дом построил, а умница купил.
        Fools build houses and wise men buy them.

281 Дурак дурака хвалит.
One fool praises another.

282 Дурак дураком остается.
Fools will be fools still.

283 Дурак пир устроил, а умница наелся.
Fools make feasts, wise men eat them.

284 Дурак торгует когда базар кончится.
When a fool has bethought himself, the market's over.

285 Дурака пошлешь, а за ним сам пойдешь.
(Умного послав - ожидай, а за безумным сам ступай.)
He that sends a fool means to follow him.

286 Дуракам во всем (везде) (всегда) счастье.
Fortune favors fools.

287* Дуракам закон не писан.
[For fools no law is written.]
Forbid a fool a thing and that he'll do.
As the fool thinks, so the bell clinks.

288 Дураку все смех на уме.
A fool is ever laughing.
Too much laughter discovers folly.

289   Заставь дурака Богу молиться, он и лоб разобьет (расшибет).
[Force a fool to pray and he'll crack his forehead.]
He would fall on his back and break his nose.
The idiot bakes snow in the oven and expects ice cream pie.

290   Один дурак в час спросит больше чем десять мудрецов сумеют ответить за год.
A fool can ask more in an hour than a wise man can answer in seven years.

291   Пошли дурака за водой, он огня несет.
[Send a fool for water and he'll fetch fire.]
I ask for a fork and you bring me a rake.

292   С дураком свяжешься, сам дурак будешь.
[Deal with a fool and become a fool yourself.]
When you argue with a fool, that makes two.
He is not the fool that the fool is, but he that with the fool deals.

293   Старого дурака ничем не исправить.
There's no fool to the (like an) old fool.

294   Тот дурак кто говорит не так.
He who thinks he is wise is a fool.

| | 295 | У дурака дурацкая и речь. |
| | | The mouth of fools pours out foolishness. |

| | 296 | Услужливый дурак опаснее врага. |
| | | A rash friend is worse than a foe. |

| **Дух** | 297 | Дух бодр, да плоть немощна. |
| | | The spirit is willing but the flesh is weak. |

Душа	298*	Чужая душа - потемки.
		(В чужую душу не влезешь.)
		[Dark is the mind of a stranger.
		(You can't get into someone else's heart.)]
		You can look in the eyes but not in the heart.
		You can't tell a book by its cover. Cf. 104

Дым	299*	Дыма без огня не бывает.
		(Где дым там и огонь.)
		No smoke without fire.
		Where there's smoke, there's fire.

	300	Любить тепло, потерпеть и дым.
		(Кто в кони пошел, тот и воду вози.)
		(Пошел в попы, служи и панихиды.)
		[If you like the heat, you must bear the smoke.
		(If you want to be a horse / priest, you must carry water / do funerals.)]
		If you don't like the heat, stay out of the kitchen.

	301	По дыму над баней пару не угодаешь. You cannot judge a tree (book) by its bark (cover).
Дыра	302	Штопай дыру пока невелика. (Берегись бед пока их нет.) [Plug a hole while it is small. (Prepare for trouble ere it comes.)] *A stitch in time saves nine.* *Prevent rather than repent.*
Дьявол	303	Воздавай должное и дьяволу. Give the devil his due.

E

Еда	304*	Каков в еде, таков в труде.

[As he eats, so he works.]

Work while you work and play while you play.

Keep your shop and your shop will keep you.

Если	305*	Если бы да кабы, то во рту росли бы грибы

(бобы) (+ и был бы не рот - а целый огород).

[If it weren't for the ifs, mushrooms (beans) would grow in my mouth (+ my mouth would not be a mouth but an orchard).]

If if's and an's were pots and pans, there'd be no trade for tinkers.

If my aunt had been a man, she'd have been my uncle.

Есть	306	Есть нета лучше.

Better aught than nought.

Ж

Ждать	307	Все приходит вовремя для того кто умеет ждать. Everything comes to him who waits.
	308	Ждать да догонять - нет хуже. [Nothing is worse than having to wait and catch up.] *A watched pot never boils.*
Желать	309	Всего желать - всего потерят. All covet, all lose.
	310	Не все сбывается что желается. [Not all materializes that is hoped for.] *If wishes were horses, beggars might ride.*
Железо	311*	Куй железо пока горячо (кипит). Strike while the iron is hot.
Жена	312	Жене и мельнице всегда довольно не бывает. Mills and wives are ever wanting.
	313	Женою доброю и муж честен. A good wife makes a good husband.
	314	Жену выбирай не глазами а ушами. Choose a wife by your ear rather than your eye.

315 За мужем жена всегда госпожа.
He that has a wife has a master.

316 Первая жена от Бога, вторая от человека, а третья от дьявола.
The first wife is matrimony, the second company, and the third heresy.

Жениться 317* Без меня меня женили.
[They married me off without me.]
The absent are always in the wrong.

318 Женишься раз, а наплачешься век.
Marry in haste, repent at leisure.

319 Не женат, не человек.
A man without a wife is but half a man.
He that has not a wife is not yet a complete man.

Жизнь 320 Где жизнь там и надежда.
(Пока дышу/живу - надеюсь.)
While there's life, there's hope.

321* Жизнь (век) прожить (пережить) - не поле перейти (что море переплыть).
[Living life (a lifetime) is not like just crossing a field (is like crossing the sea).]
Life is not a bed of roses.
(Life is a pilgrimage. Life is a voyage that's homeward bound.)

Жить   322   Где жить, там (тем) и слыть (богам и молиться).

(В какой народ приедешь, такую и шапку наденешь.)

[Heed (worship) the customs (gods) of where you live.

(Don the cap of the people you're with.)]

When in Rome, do as the Romans.

Whose bread I eat, his song I sing. **Cf.** 507

323   Живи и жить давай другим.

(Сам живи и другим не мешай.)

Live and let live.

324   Жить надейся а умирать готовься.

Plan your life as though you were going to live forever, but live today as if you were going to die tomorrow.

325   Жить страшнее чем умереть.

'Tis more brave to live than to die.

326   Кто хорошо живет, тот долго живет.

(Не тот живет больше кто живет дольше.)

He lives long that lives well.

It's not how long but how well you live.

Better to live well than long.

327* Поживем - увидим.
[Let's live and see.]
Time will tell.
Wait till we see how the cat jumps.

Жук   328   В поле (степи) и жук мясо.
[In the field (steppe), even a beetle is meat.]
Better a louse (mouse) in the pot than no flesh at all.

3

Зависть	329	Лучше быть у других в зависти нежели в кручине. Better envied than pitied.
	330	У зависти глаза велики. Nothing sharpens sight like envy.
Завтра	331*	Не откладывай до завтра что можешь сделать сегодня. Never put off till tomorrow what may be done today.
Закон	332	Закон как паутина - шмель (шершень) проскочит, а муха увязнет (увязает). Laws catch flies but let hornets go free.
Занять	333	Как занял, так и плати. Pay with the same dish you borrow.
Запас	334	Запас беды не чинит. Store *is no sore* [does not do harm].
Запрос	335	Запрос в карман не лезет. (За спрос денег не берут.) [Asking won't reach into your pocket.] *There is no harm in asking.* It costs nothing to ask.

Заяц	336*	За двумя зайцами погонишься (гонять), ни одного не поймаешь (поймать). If you run after two hares, you will catch neither.
	337	По заячьему следу доходят до медвежей берлоги. [The hare's tracks may lead you the the bear's den.] *If you begin with a common pin, you will end up with a silver bowl.* *Use the little to get to the big. Cf.156*
Здоровье	338	Здоровье дороже (богатства) (всего) (золота). Health is better than wealth. Good health is priceless.
Здравие	339*	Зачал (начали) за здравие (гладью), а свел за упокой (кончали гадью). (Взлетел орлом, прилетел голубем.) [He (they) began with "long live" (well) but ended with "rest in peace" (badly). (He took off an eagle but landed a pigeon.)] *A sweet beginning with a sour end.* *Go up like a rocket and come down like a stick.* *Cf. 421*
Земля	340	В своей земле (избе) никому пророком не быть. No man is a prophet in his own country.

341   Своя земля и в горсти мила.
[A handful of dirt is pleasing if its your own land.]
Home is home though it ever be so homely.

Зло   342   Злом зла не поправишь.
(Кривого/кривое кривым не исправишь.)
Two wrongs don't make a right.
Never do evil for evil.
Never do evil hoping that good will come of it.

343*   Из двух зол выбирай меньшее.
Choose the lesser of two evils.

Знать   344*   Много (все) будешь знать, скоро состаришься.
(Меньше знать, больше спать.)
Increase your knowledge and *increase your griefs* [you'll soon get old]. [(Know less and sleep more.)]
Much science, much sorrow. **Cf.** 531

Золотник   345*   Мал золотник, да дорог.
[The *zolotnik* is small, but valuable.]
The best things come in small packages.

Золото   346   Испытай золото огнем, а дружбу деньгами.
Gold is tested by fire, men by gold.

347*   Не все то золото что блестит.
All that glitters is not gold.

Зуб   348   Не волчий зуб, так лисий хвост.
[If the wolf's fang cannot, the fox's tail shall.]
If the lion's skin cannot, the fox's shall.

И

Игра 349 В игре да в дороге узнают людей.
In sports and journeys men are known.

Иголка 350* Куда иголка, туда и нитка.
[Where the needle goes, the thread follows.]
The appurtenance must follow the main part.

Игумен 351 Не всяк игумен (монах) на ком клобук.
(Не делает ряса/платье монахом.)
The cowl does not make the monk.

Изба 352 Из избы сор не выноси.
[Do not take your filth out of your house.]
Do not wash your dirty linen in public.

353 Не красна изба углами, а красна пирогами.
[The beauty of a house lies not in its walls but its pies.]
A house is a fine house when good folks are within.

354 У каждой избушки есть погремушки.
(Под каждой крышей свои мыши.)
[Every house has its rattles.
(There are mice under every roof.)]
There is a skeleton in every house (cupboard).

Измена	355	Измену любят а изменнику ненавидят.
		We love the treason but we hate the traitor.

Искать   356*   Кто ищет, тот найдет.
The one who seeks is the one who finds.
Seek and you shall find.

Искра   357   От искры сыр бор загорается.
(От малой искры велик пожар делается.)
A little spark kindles a great fire.
Of a small spark, a great fire.

К

Казак   358*   Терпи казак (горе), атаман(ом) будешь.
[Be patient Cossack and you'll be a chieftain.]
Patient men win the day.

Калач   359   В чужих руках калач слаще (ломоть велик) (всегда пирог шире).
(Чужой ломоть больше всегда.)
[In another's hands, the loaf is sweeter (bigger).
(Another's portion is always bigger.)]
Our neighbor's cow (ground) yields better milk (corn) than ours.
The grass is greener (on the other side). **Cf.** 941

Камень   360*   Под лежачий камень (и) вода не течет (плывет).
(На одном месте и камень мохом обростет.)
[Water never flows under a motionless stone.
(The motionless stone gathers moss.]
The rolling stone gathers no moss.
Too much rest is rust.

Капля   361*   Капля (по капле и) (вода) камень долбит.
Constant dripping wears away the stone.

362   По капельке море, по зернышку ворох.
[Drops make the sea, and grains a heap.]
Little drops of water, little grains of sand make the mighty ocean and pleasant land. **Cf.** 542

Карась   363   Не поймав карася, поймаешь щуку.
What we lose in the *hake* [carp], we shall have in the *herring* [pike].

Карта   364   Не везет в картах, везет в любви.
Unlucky at cards, lucky in love.

Кафтап   365   Крой кафтан, а к старому примеривай.
[Pattern the new suit on the old.]
Cut your coat according to your cloth.

Каша   366*   Кашу маслом не испортишь.
(Много добра не надоест.)
[Butter won't ruin *kasha*.]
You can never have too much of a good thing. **Cf.** 942

367   Овсяная (оржаная) (ржаная) каша сама себя хвалит.
[Oatmeal (barley) (buckwheat) porridge praises itself.]
The proof of the pudding is in the eating.

368* Сам заварил кашу - сам и расхлебывай.
(Что испек, то и кушай.)
As you brew, so must you drink.
As you bake, so shall you eat.

Киев 369 В огороде бузина а в Киеве дядька.
[Elderberries in the yard and an uncle in Kiev.] *i.e. a non-sequitur.*
This is for that and butter is for fish.

370* Язык до Киева доведет.
[Your tongue will get you to Kiev.]
Who has a tongue will find his way.
He who uses his tongue will reach his destination.

Клин 371* Клин (кол) клином (колом) выбивают (вышибается).
One nail (peg) drives out another.

Кобель 372 Черного кобеля не вымоешь до бела.
[You cannot wash a black mare white.]
A crow is never the whiter for washing herself often.

Козел 373 Стар козел да крепки рога.
(У старого козла крепка рога.)
Old oxen have stiff horns.

Козявка	374	Всякая козявка лезет в букашки. (Всякая кляча мнит себя рысаком.) [Every gnat (nag) yearns to be (thinks itself) a bug (thoroughbred).] *Every sprat nowadays calls itself a herring.* *Every ass thinks himself worthy to stand among the king's horses.*
Колесо	375	Худое колесо больше (громче) скрипит. The worst wheel of a cart creaks most (makes the most noise).
Колодец	376*	Не плюй в (чужой) колодец, пригодится воды напиться. Do not spit into the well you may have to drink of.
Колокольня	377	Каждый смотрит со своей колокольни. [Everyone looks out from his own belfry.] *As a man is, so he sees.*
	378	Отзвонил, (да) и с колокольни долой (прочь). [Once the bell is rung, leave the belfry.] *When the job is well done, you can hang up the hammer.*
Конец	379*	Конец всему делу венец. (Конец дело венчает/хвалит). The end crowns all (the work).

380   Начиная дело о конце размышляй (думай).
(Не смотри на начало, смотри на конец.)
Think on the end before you begin.
Begin nothing until you have considered how it is to
be finished.

Конь   381*   Конь о четырех ногах, (да) и тот спотыкается.
(И на доброго коня бывает спотычка.)
A horse stumbles that has four legs.
It is a good horse that never stumbles.

382*   Дареному   (даровому)   коню   в   зубы   не
смотрят.
Don't look a gift horse in the mouth.

383   Конь конем покупают.
He that has a *goose* [horse], will *get a goose* [buy a
horse].

384   Пришел коня ковать а кузня сгорела.
[Come to shoe the horse after the forge has burned
down.]
*It's too late to lock the stable door once the horse
has been stolen.*

385   Чей конь, того и воз.
(Чей берег, того и рыба.)
(Чья земля, того и хлеб.)
Possession is nine points of the law.

Копейка	386	Ближняя копеечка дороже дальнего рубля. (Бывает копейка дороже рубля.) A penny at a pinch is worth a pound.
	387*	Копейка рубль бережет. (Без копейки рубля нет.) [No *ruble* without a *kopek*.] Take care of the *pence* [kopeks] and the *pounds* [rubles] will take care of themselves.
Корабль	388*	Большому кораблю - большое (и) плавание. A great ship asks deep waters.
Корова	389*	Бодливой корове Бог рог не дает. [God bestows not horns upon an ill-tempered cow.] *Curst cow has short horns.*
	390	Корова черна, да молоко у ней бело. [The cow is black, but its milk is white.] *A black hen lays a white egg.*
	391	Та ведь хороша была корова к молоку, которая умерла. (Что имеем - не храним, а потерявши - плачем.) [The one that died was a great milk cow.] *The worth of a thing is best known by the want of it.* *The fish that escapes is the biggest fish of all.*

392   У корове молоко на языке.
You don't get more out of a thing than you put into it.

Коса   393   Коси коса пока роса.
[Mow while the dew is down.]
Make hay while the sun shines.

394*   Нашла коса на камень.
[The scythe has struck a stone.]
The irresistible force has met the immovable object.

Костер   395   Хорошо около костра щепы подбирать.
[It's nice to gather chips near the fire.]
It is best to sit near the fire when the chimney smokes.

Кот   396   Битому коту лишь лозу покажи.
A beaten *dog* [cat] escheweth the whip. *Cf.* 139, 502

397   Кот охотник до рыбы, да воды боится.
The cat would eat fish and would not wet her feet.

398*   Не все коту масленица (+ бывает и великий пост).
[It's not just Carnival for the cat (+ Lent also comes).]
Christmas comes but once a year.
After Christmas comes Lent.

Кошелек	399	Старыми руками трудно кошелек развязывать.

Кошелек   399   Старыми руками трудно кошелек развязывать.
[Old hands don't easily untie the purse strings.]
The older the bird, the more unwillingly it parts with its feathers.

Кошка   400   Где нет кошки, там мыши резвятся.
(Без кота мышам масленица/раздолье.)
When the cat's away, the mice will play.

             401*   Знает кошка чье мясо съела.
[The cat knows whose meat it ate.]
You cannot hide from your conscience.

             402   Знай кошка (кошурка) свое лукошко (свою конурку).
[A cat (dog) should know its basket (kennel).]
Everybody ought to know his own business the best.

             403   Кошка (лиса) (сова) спит, а мышей (кур) видит.
[The cat (fox) (owl) sees mice (chickens) in her sleep.]
The net of the sleeper catches fish.
All thoughts of a turtle are turtle, of a rabbit, rabbit. **Cf.** 424

404   Кошке игрушки, а мышки слезки.
[Playthings for the cat, but tears for the mouse.]
It is no play where one weeps and another laughs.
What's good for one may be bad for another. **Cf.**
14, 579

405*   Кошку в мешке не покупают.
(За очи коня не купят/покупают).
One doesn't buy a *pig* [cat] in a poke.
Never buy *anything* [a horse] before you see it.

406   Ночью все кошки серы (черны) (все лошадки
вороные).
(Ночью все дороги гладки.)
All cats (horses) are black (grey) in the night.
All *shapes, all colors,* [roads] are *alike* [smooth] in
the dark.

407   Отзовутся   (отольются)   кошке   (волку)
(медведью)   мышкины   (овечьи)   (коровьи)
слезки.
[The cat (wolf) (bear) will pay (cry) for the mouse's
(sheep's) (cow's) tears.]
He that mischief hatches, mischief catches.
Curses, like chickens, come home to roost.

Красивый	408*	Не родись красивым (ни умен ни красив), а родись счастливым (счастлив).
		Better born lucky than *rich* (wise) [pretty].
Красота	409	Красота и глупость часто бывают купно.
		Beauty and folly go often in company .
	410	Снаружи красота, внитри пустота.
		(Сверху мило, внутри гнило.)
		Fair without, false within.
		Fair face, foul heart.
		Beauty is only skin deep.
Краткость	411	Краткость - сестра таланта.
		Brevity is the *soul of wit* [sister of talent].
Кривой	412	У кривого один глаз, да видит больше всех нас.
		He that has but one eye, sees the better for it.
Крик	413	Криком ничего не сделаешь (изба не рубится).
		(Шумом праву не быть.)
		[Shouting never accomplished anything (built a house).]
		Those who are right need not talk loudly.
		Some think the louder they shout, the more persuasive their argument is. Striking manners are bad manners.

Купить	414*	За что купил, за то и продаю. [I'm selling at the same price I bought.] *Speak as you find.* *Wrong hearing makes wrong rehearsing.*
Кувшин	415	Повадился кувшин по воду ходить, там ему и голову сломить. The pitcher goes so often to the well that it is broken at last.
Кузнец	416	Всяк (всякий) кузнец своего счастья. Every man is architect of his own fortune.
Кузня	417	Все кузни исходил, а не кован воротился. Send a fool to market and a fool he will return.
Кулик	418	Всяк кулик на своем болоте велик. [Every sandpiper is great in his own swamp.] *Every dog is valiant at his* *own door. Cf. 615, 797*
	419*	Каждый (всякий) кулик (купец) (цыган) свое болото (свой товар) (свою кобылу) хвалит. Every peddler [(sandpiper) (gypsy) praises his *needles* [ware (swamp) (mare)]. *Each priest praises his own relics.* *Every doctor thinks his pills the best.*

420   Кулик не велик, а все-таки птица.
[The sandpiper is small, but a bird just the same.]
Every fish is not a sturgeon.
All flesh is not venison.

Кум   421   Пошел (зашел) к куме, да засел в тюрьме.
[Set out to my godfather but wound up in jail.]
A bad end from a good beginning.
You began (begin) better than you end. **Cf.** 339

Купить   422   У голодной куме, хлеб на уме.
[The hungry godfather has bread on his mind.]
The hungry man often talks of bread (sees meat from afar).

Курица   423   Бесплодная курица много кудахчет.
[The barren hen cackles often.]
You cackle often, but never lay an egg.

424   Голодной курице (все) просо снится.
[A hungry chicken dreams of millet.]
Pigs dream of acorns and the goose of maize. **Cf.** 403

425   И у курицы (воробья) есть сердце.
[Even a chicken (swallow) has a heart.]
The fly has her spleen, the ant her gall.

426   От худой курицы худые яйцы.
Of an evil crow an evil egg. *Cf.* 986

Л

Ласточка	427	Одна ласточка лета не делает (весны не приносит). One swallow makes not a summer (spring).
Лгать	428	(Кто) вчера соврал (солгал), тому и завтра не поверят (а сегодня лгуном обзывают). (Лжецу и в правде не верят.) He that once deceives, is ever suspected. A liar is not believed when he speaks the truth.
	429	Кто лжет, тот и крадет. He that will lie, will steal.
Лев	430	Льва сонного не буди. Wake not a sleeping lion.
Легко	431	Что легко наживается, легко и проживается. (Наживать долго, а прожить скоро.) Easy come, easy go. *Narrow gathered, widely spent.*
Лежачий	432*	Лежачего не бьют. You don't kick a man when he is down.

| Лекарство | 433 | Противное лекарство приятнее болезни.
Bitter pills may have blessed effects.
Good medicine always tastes bitter. |

Лекарство 433 Противное лекарство приятнее болезни.
Bitter pills may have blessed effects.
Good medicine always tastes bitter.

Лень 434 Лень добра не делает.
(Лень до добра не доводит.)
Of idleness comes no goodness.
Trouble springs from idleness.

Лес 435 В лесу лес не ровен, в миру - люди.
It takes all kinds of trees to make a forest.
It takes all sorts to make a world.

436* Дальше в лес, больше дров.
The further in [the woods], *the deeper* [the more logs].

437* Кто в лес, кто по дрова.
[Some go into the woods, some go for wood.]
There are more ways to the wood than one.
So many heads, so many wits.

438 Лес по топорищу (дереву) не плачет (тужит).
The axe goes to the wood from whence it borrowed its helve.

439* Лес рубят - щепки летят.
   (Где дрова рубят, там и щепы летят.)
   [Where the wood is chopped, the chips will fly.] .
   You can't make an omelette without breaking eggs.
   He that would have eggs must endure the cackling
   of hens. **Cf.** 997

Лето 440* Готовь летом сани а зимой телегу.
   [Prepare your sleigh in summer and your wagon in
   winter.]
   In fair weather prepare for foul.

  441 Опустя лето, да в лес по малину.
   [Miss summer and then go to the woods for
   raspberries.]
   Baskets after vintage.
   Come a day after the fair. **Cf.** 893

Лжец 442 Лжецу надо(бно) добрая память.
   A liar should have a good memory.

Лихо 443 Лихо не лежит тихо.
   [Ill never lies still.]
   Bad pennies always turn up.
   Small evils hatch quick.

Лицо 444 Лицо - зеркало души.
   (Что в сердце варится, то в лице не утаится.)
   The face is the index of the mind (heart).

| Лишний | 445 | Лишнему лишнее и надобно. |
| | | Much would have more. |

Лоб	446*	Лбом стену (стенку) не прошибешь.
		[You can't break down the wall with your head.]
		No man can flay a stone.
		You can't get blood (water) from a stone. **Cf.** 172

	447*	Что в лоб - что по лбу.
		(Кто ни поп, тот/то и батька.)
		[It's either in your face or against your face.
		(It's either a priest or a clergyman.)]
		It's either six of one or half a dozen of the other.

Ложка	448*	Дорога ложка к обеду
		(Дорого яичко к Христову/великому дню.)
		[It's nice to have a spoon (an egg) in time for dinner (Easter).]
		Slow help is no help.
		Better on time than late. **Cf.** 893

| Ложь | 449 | Ложь ложью погоняет. |
| | | One lie makes many. |

| | 450 | Ложью свет пройдешь, да не воротишься. |
| | | A liar can go round the world but cannot come back. |

| | 451 | Лучше ложь ко спасению нежели правда к погибели. |
| | | Better a lie that heals than a truth that wounds. |

Локоть	452*	Локоть близок, да не укусишь.
		The elbow is near, but try and bite it.

453 Быстрая (вода) лошадь скорее станет (до моря не доходит).
[The fast-running horse (water) tires sooner (reaches not the sea.).]
He that runs fast will not run long.

Лошадь 454 Дай глупому лошадь, так он на ней и к черту уедет.
Give a beggar a horse and he'll ride it to *death* [the devil].
Beggars mounted run their horse to death.

455 Для ленивой лошади и дуга в тягость.
A lazy horse thinks its harness heavy.

456 Которая лошадь больше везет, на ту больше и наваливают.
All lay load on the willing horse.

Лыко 457 Не всякое лыко в строку.
[Not every cord is used in the weave.]
An inch breaks no square.
Mistakes don't make haystacks.

Любовь 458 Любовь начинается с глаз.
Loving comes by looking.
Looks breed love.

459   Любовь покрывает множество грехов.
Love covers many infirmities. *Cf.* 460, 809

460*   Любовь слепа.
Love is blind. *Cf.* 459, 809

461*   От любви до ненависти один шаг.
[From love to hate is but a step.]
Love is akin to hate.
Love and hate are the two closest emotions.

462   Старая любовь долго помнится (не ржавеет).
Old love will not be forgotten.
Old love does not rust.

Люди   463   Все люди, все человеки.
We are only human.
We are all Adam's children.

464   Жили люди до нас, будут жить и после нас.
(Не нами началось/свет начался, не нами и кончится/скончается.)
[There were people before us and there will be people after us.
(The world neither began nor will it end with us).]
I'm not the first and shall not be the last.
There were brave men before Agamemnon.

465   Людей много, а человека нет.
(Много народа да мало людей.)
A crowd is not company.

466*   Свои люди - сочтемся.
[We're all friends - we'll settle up.]
It will all come right in the wash.
Friends have all things in common. **Cf.** 561

М

Макар	467	На бедного Макара все шишки валятся. [All the cones drop on poor Makar.] *An unhappy man's cart is easy to overthrow.* *The Tracy's have always the wind in their faces.* *Cf.* 25
Малый	468	Из многих малых выходит одно большое. (Великое число из единиц составляется.) (Без одной не сотня.) Many smalls make a great. Many a little makes a mickle.
	469	Кто малым не доволен, тот большого не достоин. [He that is not content with little, does not deserve much.] *He that cannot abide in a bad market, deserves not a good one.*
	470	Малые от старых учатся. (Щенок лает, от больших слышит.) [The young learn from the old. (The pup barks as it hears its elders bark.] *As the old cock crows, the young cock learns.*

Масло	471*	Маслом огонь не заливают (огня не потушишь). Pouring oil on the fire is not the way to quench it.
Мастер	472	Всяк мастер на свой лад. (У всякого молодца своя ухватка.) (Всяк своему нраву работает.) Every man (one) after his fashion.
Мать	473	Всякой матери свое дитя мило. (При матке все детки гладки.) No mother has a homely child. *Cf.* 7
Маша	474	Хороша Маша да не наша. (Хорош кус, да не для наших уст.) It's a good fish if it were caught.
Мед	475	Где мед там и муха. A fly follows the honey.
	476	Медом больше мух наловишь чем уксусом. Honey catches more flies than vinegar.
Медаль	477	У каждой медали есть оборотная сторона. Every medal has its reverse. *Cf.* 606
Медведь	478*	Два медведя в одной берлоге не уживутся. [Two bears cannot abide in one den.] *Two sparrows on one ear of corn make an ill agreement.*

479* Не поймав (убивши) медведя, не продают шкуры.
Don't sell the bear's skin before you have caught the bear.

Меньше 480* Лучше меньше, да лучше.
(Лучше в малом да удача, чем в огромном да провал.)
(Маленькое дело лучше большого безделья.)
[Better smaller but better.
(Better a small success than a huge failure.)
(Better a little business than a lot of idleness.)]
It's better to be a little wheel turning than a big wheel standing still.
A little along is better than a long none.
Better to be small and shine than to be great and cast a shadow.

Мера 481* Все хорошо в меру.
Everything in moderation.

Мертвый 482 О мертвых (покойниках) - или хорошо, или ничего (плохо не говорят).
[Of the dead, speak either well or not at all.]
Speak well of the dead.

483 Хорошо лгать на мертвого.
The dead (absent) are always wrong.

Место 484* Всему свое место.
[Everything has its place.]
A place for everything and everything in its place.

485* Не место человека красит (просвещает), а человек место.
It is not the place that honors the man, but the man that honors the place.

Метла 486* Новая метла (новый веник) чисто метет.
A new broom sweeps clean.

Меч 487 Мечом золото добывают, а меч золотом покупают.
Gold and iron are used to buy gold and iron.

Милый 488 Милые бранятся - только тешатся.
Lovers' quarrels are soon mended.

Мир 489 Если хочешь мира, будь готов к войне.
If you want peace, you must prepare for war.

490 Мир тесен.
It's a small world.

491 На весь мир мягко не постелешь.
(Одним всем/на всех не угодишь/услужишь.
[You cannot make a soft bed for everyone.]
It is hard to please all parties.
You can't please everybody.
None so good that it's good to all.

492   Худой мир лучше доброй брани (ссоры).
Better a lean peace than fat victory.

Много   493   Любишь много, люби и мало.
You must take the fat with the lean. *Cf.* 526, 732

494   Много (долго) выбирать - женатым (замужем) не бывать.
If you always say "No" you'll never be married.

Молодец   495   Молодец на (против)(среди) овец, а на (против)(среди) молодца, (и) сам овца.
[Bold against (among) sheep, but himself a sheep against (among) the bold.]
Who takes a lion when absent, fears a mouse present.
A bully is always a coward.

Молодой   496   Два раза (дважды) молодому не быть.
Youth comes but once in a lifetime.
You're only young once. *Cf.* 227

497*   Молодо - зелено (+ погулять велено).
[Young and green (+ will wander).]
Young colts will canter.
Youth will have its course.

498   Молодой - игрушки, а старый - подушки.
[Toys for the young, pillows for the old.]
Youth is a crown of roses, old age a crown of willows.

499   Молодому жениться рано, а старому поздно.
A young man should not marry yet, an old man not at all.

500   Молодые (люди) могут умереть, старики должны.
Young men may die, but old must die.

Молодость   501   Если бы молодость знала (умела), а старость могла.
If youth but knew and age but could do.
If only youth had the experience and old age had the strength.

Молоко   502*   Обжегшись на молоке (и) на воду дуешь.
[One scalded on milk will blow on water.]
A scalded cat fears hot water. **Cf.** 139, 396

Молоток   503   Лучше быть молотком чем наковальней.
It is better to be the hammer than the anvil.

504   Тяжело молоту, тяжело и наковальне.
[What's hard on the hammer will be hard on the anvil.]
What's sauce for the goose is sauce for the gander.

Молчание   505*   Молчание знак согласия.
Silence means consent.

506   Молчанием прав не будешь.
[Silence will not make you right.]
The lame tongue gets nothing.

Монастырь   507   В чужой монастырь со своим уставом не ходи.
[Go not to another's monastery with your own dogma.]
Measure not another's corn by your own bushel.
In Rome, do as the Romans. Cf. 322

Монах   508   Хватился каяться монах, как уж смерть в головах.
When the devil comes, it's too late to pray.

Море   509   Кто молиться не умеет, тот пойди на море.
He that would learn to pray, let him go to sea.

510   Море по рыбке не тужит.
[The sea grieves not for fish.]
The sea has fish for every man.

511   Хвали море, а сиди на берегу.
Praise the sea but keep on land.

Москва	512	Все дороги ведут в Москву. All roads lead to *Rome* [Moscow].
	513	Москва не сразу (вдруг) (клином) стропилась (соплась). *Rome* [Moscow] wasn't built in a day. *Cf.* 741
	514*	Москва слезам не верит. [Moscow does not believe in tears.] *Tears bring nobody back from the grave.* *Two barrels of tears will not heal a bruise. Cf.* 769
	515	Не хвались в Москву (идучи/шедши на рать), а хвались из Москвы (идучи/шедши с рати). (Не радуйся/суди по приезду, радуйся/суди по отъезду.) [Boast (praise) not on your way to Moscow (the fray) (on arriving), but on your return.] Praise in departing. Triumph not before the victory. *Cf.* 536
Мочалка	516	Мочалка с мочалкой и вяжется. [Wisp will to wisp.] *Birds of a feather flock together. Cf.* 632

Мудрец	517	Во всяком мудреце довольно простоты. (И на мудреца бывает простота.) No man is wise at all times. The wise man may sometimes play the fool.
Мудрость	518	Мудрость в голове, а не в бороде. The brains don't lie in the beard.
Мудрый	519	Мудрый (умный) слышит в (понимает и) пол(у)слова. (Умному не много слов.) A word to the wise is sufficient.
Мужик	520	Побей мужика - часы сделает. [Beat the peasant and he'll fashion a watch.] *A man can do a lot of things if he has to.*
Мука	521	Перемелется, (все) мука будет. [Eventually it will all be ground like fine flour.] *It will all come right in the wash.* **Cf.** 466
Мы	522	Кто не с нами, тот против нас. Whoever is not with us is against us.
Мысль	523	На мысле запрета нет. (С мыслей пошлин не берут.) Thought is free.

Мышь   524   Мышь сыта, мука горька.
When the *cat* [mouse] is full, the *milk* [flour] tastes sour. *Cf.* 766

525   Худа та мышь которая одну лазейку знает.
The mouse that has but one hole is quickly taken.

Н

Найти	526	Любишь найти, люби и потерять. You win a few, you lose a few. *Cf.* 493, 732
Налет	527	Гляди налет на свой полет. [Measure your lunge to your flight.] *Make not your sail too big for the ballast.* *Cf.* 223
Наружность	528	Наружность обманчива. Appearances are deceiving.
Натура	529	Натура волка в лесу гонит. [Nature drives the wolf to the woods.] *A frog cannot out of her bog.*
	530	Натура не дура. Nature (God) is no botcher.
	531	Наука - мука. Much science (learning), much sorrow. *Cf.* 344
Начало	532	Без начала и конца не бывает. Where there's no beginning there's no end. Whatever begins also ends.

	533	Все имеет начало. Everything has a beginning.
	534	Всякое начало трудно. All beginnings are hard. The first step is the hardest.
	535	Доброе начало - половина дела. (Лиха беда начало.) Well begun--half done. *The first blow is half the battle.*
	536	Не хвались началом, похвались концом. Do not boast of a thing until it is done. *Cf.* 515
Начать	537*	Умел начать, умей и кончать. Never start what you cannot finish. *Cf.* 223
Невод	538	Прежде невода рыбы не ловят. It is ill fishing before the net.
Недосол	539	Недосол на столе, (а) пересол на спине. [Undersalted on the table, oversalted on the back.] *Salt cooks bear blame, but fresh bear shame.*
Нет	540*	На нет и суда нет. [There's no choice when there's nothing.] *Beggars can't be choosers.* *A man cannot give what he hasn't got.*

Нитка	541	Длинная нитка - ленивая швея. A long thread, a lazy tailor.
	542*	С миру по нитке - голому рубаха (рубашка). [A thread from everyone will make a shirt for the needy.] *Add little to little and there will be a great heap.* *Cf.* 362
Ничего	543	Ничем ничего не сделаешь. Nothing comes of nothing.
Нищий	544	Нищий вора не боится. (Голый/нищий на голом/нищем не ищет.) The beggar may sing before the thief. No naked man is sought after to be rifled.
Новый	545	На свете ничего нового нет. Nothing new under the sun.
Нога	546	Лучше споткнуться ногою нежели словом. Better the foot slip than the tongue.
	547	Никто на свою ногу топора не опустит. No man is hurt by himself.
Нос	548	Нос вытащит - хвост увязит (завязит), хвост вытащит - нос увязит (завязит). [Pull out the beak and the tail gets stuck, pull out the tail and the beak gets stuck.] *If it's not one thing, it's another.*

Ночь	549	Темная ночь не навек. The longest night will have an end. *Cf.* 231
Ноша	550*	Своя ноша не тянет (тяжела). A burden of one's choice is not felt.
Нужда	551	Кто нужды не видал, тот и счастья не знает. One does not appreciate happiness unless one has known sorrow.
	552	Нужда дружит и кошку с собакой. [Need makes friends of cats and dogs.] *Adversity makes strange bedfellows.*
	553	Нужда закона не знает. Need (necessity) knows no law.
	554	Нужда и по воскресным дням постится. Necessity has no holiday.
	555	Нужда научит калачи есть. (Нужда учит родить/всему учит.) (Нужда острит разум.) [Need will teach one to eat *kalachi*.] Necessity is the mother of invention. Necessity sharpens *industry* [the mind]. *Cf.* 180

556   Нужда цены не знает.
[Need knows no price.]
Necessity never made a good bargain.

Нынче   557   Одно «нынче» лучше двух «завтра».
One today is worth two tomorrows.

Нянька   558*   У семи нянек (маток) дитя без глазу.
With seven nannies a child will be without eyes.
Too many cooks spoil the broth. **Cf.** 609

О

Обещать	559	Кто много обещает, тот мало дает. He that promises much, means nothing.
	560*	Обещанного три года ждут. [There's a three-year wait for what is promised.] *Promises are made to be broken.*
	561	Обещать и слово держать как небо и земля. It's one thing to promise, another to perform. *Cf.* 774
Обида	562	Лучше в обиде быть (мучиться), чем в обидчиках (мучить). Better to suffer ill than to do ill. *Better to be a martyr than a confessor.*
Обман	563	Обман спасительный лучше истины гибельной. Better a lie that heals than a truth that wounds.
Объять	564	Нельзя объять необъятное. [One cannot embrace the unembraceable.] *No one is bound to do impossibilities.*
Обычай	565	Равные (разные) обычаи, крепкая любовь. Likeness causes liking. (Opposites attract.) *Cf.* 632

Овца	566	Куда одна овца (один баран), туда и все стадо. One sheep follows another.
	567	Овец не стало, и на коз честь. [When the sheep are gone, the goats have the honor.] *If you can't get a horse, ride a cow.*
	568*	Одна паршивая (шелудивая) овца все стадо портит. One scabbed sheep will mar a whole flock. *Cf.* 987
	569*	С паршивой (лихой) овцы (собаки) хоть шерсти клок. [From a bad sheep (dog) get at least a clump of wool (fur).] *Make the best of a bad situation.* *Something is better than nothing.*
	570	Сделайся овцою а волки будут. He that makes himself a sheep shall be eaten by the wolf.
Овчинка	571*	Овчинка (шкура) выделки не стоит. (Игра не стоит свеч.) The game isn't worth the candle.

Огонь	572	В сене огня не скроешь.

Огонь   572   В сене огня не скроешь.
(Солома с огнем не улежит.)
Fire cannot be hidden in straw (flax).
Fire and flax agree not.

573*   Из огня (сохи) да в полымя (борону).
[From the flame (plough) into the fire (harrow).]
From the frying pan into the fire. **Cf.** 120

574   С огнем шутить не надо.
Don't play with fire.

Одежда   575*   По одежке (платье) встречают, по уму провожают.
[One is received according to one's dress and sent off according to one's wit.]
Good clothes open all doors.
Clothes make the man.

576*   По одежке (кроватке) протягивай ножки.
Stretch your legs according to your coverlet.

Один   577*   Один в поле не воин (ратник).
[One man in a field does not make a warrior.]
One man is no man.

578*   Один за всех, все за одного.
One for all and all for one.

579 Одни (несчастные) плачут а другие (счастливые) скачут.
(Один радуется а другой плачет.)
(Одному сбылось, а другому не удалось.)
[Some (the unlucky) cry, some (the lucky) skip and jump.]
Some win, some lose.
There's no great banquet but some fare ill.
Some have the hap, others stick in the gap. **Cf.** 14, 404

580 Одни сеют, другие жнут.
Some sow, others reap.

Око 581 Око видит далеко, а мысль (ум) еще дальше.
The eye looks but the mind sees. *May 2006*

582 Око за око, зуб за зуб.
An eye for an eye and a tooth for a tooth.

Опыт 583 Опыт - лучший учитель.
Experience is the best teacher.

Опытность 584 Опытность нередко заменяет учение.
Experience is often a substitute for learning.

Орел 585 Орлом мух не ловят (орел мух не ловит).
Eagles catch no flies.

	586	Старого орла трудно на гнезде поймать. [An old eagle is not easily caught in his roost.] *An old fox is not easily snared.*
Орех	587	Не разгрызешь (раскуся) ореха, так не съешь ядра (о зерне не толкуй). He that will eat the kernel, must crack the nut.
Осел	588	Осла пригласили на свадьбу - возить дрова и воду. [The ass was asked to the wedding, but to haul logs and water.] *The parrot has fine feathers but he doesn't go to the dance.*
Остаток	589*	Остатки сладки. [Leftovers are sweet.] That which is last is best. *The nearer the bone, the sweeter the flesh.* *Seconds are the gold dust of time.*
Осторожность	590	Осторожность - мать безопасности (мудрости). Caution is the parent of safety.
Отвага	591	Отвага - половина победы. A bold heart is half the battle.

Отец	592	Каков отец (батька), таковы у него и детки. Like father, like son.
	593	Отец рыбак - дети в воду смотрят. [A fisherman's children look to the sea.] *He that comes of a hen must scrape.*
	594	Отцы ели клюкву а у детей оскомина на зубах. [The fathers ate the cranberries and the children are left with the aftertaste.] *Adam ate the apple and our teeth still ache.*
Отечество	595	Там и отечество где жить добро. Where it is well with me, there is my country.
Охота	596	На охоту ехать - собак кормить. [Feed the dogs if you want to hunt.] *Thatch your roof before the rain begins.* *Have not thy cloak to make when it begins to rain.*
	597	Охота не работа. [Willingness is not work.] *It is easy to do what one's self wills.*
	598*	Охота пуще неволи. [Compulsion is worse than coercion.] *Desire has no rest.*

Mar 2000

Ошибка

599   Ошибка в фальшь не ставится.
       [An error is not held against you.]
       Erring is not cheating.

600*   На ошибках (ошибками) учатся.
       Failure teaches success.
       We learn by our mistakes.

П

Павел	601	У всякого Павла своя правда. [Every Paul has his own truth.] *Every man to his own opinion.*
Павлин	602	Хорош павлин, да ногами худ. The peacock has fair feathers but foul feet.
Падать	603	Сколь часто падаешь, столь часто вставай. (Хоть падать, да не лежать.) [As often as you fall, get up.] *Success comes in rising every time you fall.* *Never say die.*
Палец	604*	Дай ему палец - он всю руку откусит. Give a clown your finger and he will take your hand.
Палка	605	Без палки нет учения. Spare the rod and spoil the child.
	606*	У палки (всякой вещи) два конца. [A stick has two ends.] *There are two sides to every question.* *When you pick up a stick at one end, you also pick up the other end.* *Cf.* 477

Пан	607*	Либо пан, либо пропал.

Пан   607*   Либо пан, либо пропал.
(Либо/или грудь в крестах, либо/или голова в кустах.)
(Либо/или в стремя ногой, либо/или в пень головой.)
[Either a gentleman or nothing.
(Either a cross on your chest/foot in the stirrup or your head in the shrubs/tree stump.)
It's either win all or lose all.
Either win the saddle or lose the horse. **Cf.** 722

Париж   608   Осла хоть в Париж, все будет рыж.
(Гусь за море полетел - гусь, а не лебедь и назад прилетел.)
If an ass goes a-traveling, he'll not come home a horse.

Пастух   609   У семи пастухов не стадо.
(Семеро капралов, один рядовой.)
[Seven shepherds - no flock.
(Seven corporals, one private.)]
Too many commanders cause confusion in the ranks.
Too many chiefs and not enough braves.
Too many Eskimos, too few seals. **Cf.** 558

Пень   610   Наряди пень, и пень будет хорош.
Dress up a stick and it does not appear to be a stick.

Перо 611 В одно перо и птица не родится.
(Раз на раз не приходится.)
[Not all birds have the same feathers.]
No like is the same.

612* Что написано пером - не вырубишь топором.
[What the pen has writ, no axe can rend.]
The pen is mightier than the sword.
The written letter (word) remains.

Песня 613* Из песни слова не выкинешь.
[You can't drop a word from a song.]
Tell the truth, the whole truth and nothing but the truth.
Half the truth is often a great lie.

Петр 614 Далеко кулику до Петрова дня.
[The sandpiper has a long wait till St. Peter's Day.]
It's a long way to Tiparary.

Петух 615 Всяк петух (всякая курица) на своем пепелище хозяин.
(В своем курятнике петух хозяин.)
A cock is bold (master) on his own dunghill (of his coop). *Cf.* 418, 797

616 Незван в пир не ходит.
Don't go if you're uninvited.

Пирог	617	Один пирог два раза не съешь.
		(С одного вола двух шкур/две шкуры не дерут.)
		You can't eat the same bread (pie) twice.
		You cannot have your cake and eat it.
	618	Худ пирог, да съелся.
		[It was a bad pie, but it was eaten anyway.]
		No good horse of a bad color.
Платье	619*	Береги платье снову а честь смолоду.
		[Take care of your dress from when its new and your honor from youth.]
		Learn young, learn fair.
		The mark must be made in youth.
Плод	620*	Запретный плод сладок.
		(Чего нельзя, того и хочется.)
		Forbidden fruit is sweet.
Победа	621	Победа требует прилежания.
		Victory belongs to the most persevering.
Победитель	622	Победителей не судят.
		[The victors are not judged.]
		Success is never blamed.
Повар	623	Не все те повары у кого ножи долгие.
		Not everyone who carries a long knife is a cook.

624   Повар с голоду не умрет.
[A cook never starves to death.]
A three years' drought will not starve a cook.

Повешенный 625   В доме повешенного не говорят о веревке.
Name not a halter in the house of the hanged.

626   Кому быть повешенному, тот не утонет.
(Родись плясуном и будешь плясать.)
He that is born to be hanged, shall never be drowned. *Cf.* 113

Повидаться 627*   С кем поведешься (повидаешься), от того и наберешься.
A person is reflected in the friends he chooses.
A man is known by his friends. *Cf.* 274

Повиноваться 628   Кто не умеет повиноваться, тот не умеет повелевать.
No man can be a good ruler, unless he has first been ruled.

Повторение 629*   Повторение мать учения.
Repetition is the mother of learning (skill).

Подарок 630*   Не дорог подарок, дорога любоиь.
It's not the gift that counts, but the thought behind it.

	631	От того кто не мил и подарок постыл. A wicked man's gift has a touch of its master.
Подобный	632	Подобный подобного любит. (Кто на кого похож, тот с тем и схож.) Likeness causes liking. Like will to like. *Birds of a feather flock together. Cf.* 516, 565
Под- слушивать	633	Кто подслушивает, слышит себе неприятное. Listen at the keyhole and you'll hear bad news about yourself.
Поздно	634*	Лучше поздно чем никогда. Better late than never.
Поиграть	635	Чем поиграешь, тем и ушибешься (зашибешься). [What you play with will get you.] *They who play with edged tools must expect to be cut.* *You may play with the bull till you get his horn in your eye.*
Полковник	636	Жил - полковник, помер - покойник. [He lived a colonel but died a corpse.] *Today a man, tomorrow none.*
Положить	637	Подальше положишь, поближе возмешь. [The farther you put it, the nearer you'll find it.] *Fast (safe) (sure) bind, fast (safe) (sure) find.*

Полузнание	638	Полузнание хуже незнания. (Недоученный хуже неученого.) [Half-knowing is worse than not knowing.] Better untaught than ill-taught. *A little knowledge (learning) is a dangerous thing.*
Поп	639	Иной (кто) любит попа, другой (кто) попадью, а иной (кто) попову дочку. [One loves the priest, another the priest's wife, and another the daughter.] *There's no accounting for tastes.* *All meat's to be eaten, all maids to be wed.* **Cf.** 99
	640	Каков (за что) поп (игумен), таков(ы) (за то) и приход (братья). Like priest, like people.
	641	Кто любит попа, тот ласкает и попову собаку. [If you love the priest, be nice to his dog.] *He that loves the tree, loves the branch.*
Попасться	642	Попался, который кусался. The biter bit.
Попытка	643*	Попытка не пытка (шутка) (+ а спрос не беда). There's no harm in trying.
Порода	644	Не хвались породой - чужим хвастаешься. He who boasts of his descent, praises the deeds of another.

Поручиться 645 Кто поручится тот и мучится.
He that goes a-borrowing, goes a-sorrowing.

Порча 646 Без порчи (не испортивши) и дела не сделаешь.
(Не ошибается тот, кто ничего не делает.)
He who makes no mistakes, makes nothing.
He who never made a mistake, never made anything.

Пословица 647 Пословица не мимо ходит (молвится) (во век не сломится).
Common proverb seldom lies.
Old saws speak truth.

648 Пословицу не обойти и не объехать.
Proverbs cannot be contradicted.

Посол 649 Посла ни секут, ни рубят, только милуют.
Messengers should neither be beheaded nor hanged [only pardoned].

Поспешность 650 Поспешность нужна только блох ловить.
(Спешить хорошо лишь блох ловить.)
Nothing must be done hastily but killing of fleas.

Постлать 651 Как кто постелет, так и выспится.
(Как постелишь, так и поспишь.)
As you make your bed, so you must lie on it. *Cf.* 753

Посудина	652	Битая посудина два века живет. [Chipped china lasts two centuries.] Ill vessels seldom miscarry. *Nought is never in danger.*
Потереться	653	Около чего потрешься, того и наберешься. He that has to do with what is foul never comes away clean. *Cf.* 731
Почет	654	Больше почет, больше хлопот Great honors are great burdens.
Правда	655	В ногах правды нет. [No truth in standing.] *It is as cheap sitting as standing.*
	656	Говорить правду - (по)терять дружбу. (Не говори правду, не теряй дружбу.) [(Don't) tell the truth and lose a friend.] *Truth finds foes where it makes none.* *All truths must not be told at all times.*
	657	На правду мало слов. Truth needs not the ornament of many words. Truth gives a short answer.
	658*	Правда глаза колет. [Truth stings the eyes.] *The truth hurts.* *Truth tastes bitter.*

659   Правда диковиннее вымысла.
Truth is stranger than fiction.

660   Правда суда не боится.
Truth fears no trial.

661   Правда хорошо, а счастье лучше.
Better to be happy than right.
Better be born lucky than wise. *Cf.* 859

662   Правда шутки не любит.
It is ill jesting with the truth.
The truest jests sound worst in guilty ears.

663   Правду красить нет нужды.
Truth has no need of rhetoric (figures).

Правило   664*   Нет правила без исключений.
There is no general rule without some exception.

Праздник   665*   Будет и на нашей улице праздник.
(Авось и к нам взойдет солнышко на двор.)
[Our street to will have its fair.
(Perhaps the sun will shine in our yard too.)]
Our day will come.
Every dog has its day.

	666	Ленивому всегда праздник. Every day is a holiday with sluggards.
Праздность	667	Праздность есть мать пороков. Idleness is the root of all evil.
Предел	668	Всему есть свой предел. There's a limit to everything.
Привычка	669	.Привычка вторая натура (другая природа). Custom is a second nature.
Пример	670*	Дурные примеры заразительные. (Глупость заразительна.) Nothing so contagious (infectious) as a bad example. *One fool makes many (a hundred).*
Природа	671	Гони природу в дверь, а она в окно войдет (влетит). [Drive nature out the door and she'll come (fly) back through the window.] *You can drive out nature with a pitchfork, but she keeps on coming back.*
	672	Природа натуру одолевает. Nature passes nurture.
Причина	673	Без причины ничего не бывает. There is a reason for everything. *There's reason in all things.* **Cf.** 706

Промедление 674   Промедление смерти подобно.
[Delaying is like dying.]
Kill time and time will kill you.

Простота 675   Простота хуже воровства.
[It's worse to be a fool than a thief.]
Better be a rogue than a fool.

Птица 676*   Видна (знать) птица(у) по перьям, а
человек(а) (молодца) по речам.
(Видна птица/сокол по полету.)
The bird is known by its note, the man by his words.

677   Всякая птица свое гнездо любит.
Every bird likes his own nest best.

678   Коготок увяз - всей птички пропасть.
[A little claw stuck and the whole bird is lost.]
A little stone in the way overturns a great wain.
Small leaks sink big ships.

679   Мало по малу птичка свивает гнездо.
Little by little the bird builds his nest.

680   Малые птички свивают малые гнезда.
Small birds make little nests.

681 Птичка не велика, да ноготок востер.
(Ящерка маленька, да зубы остреньки.)
No viper so little but has its venom.

682 Худая та птица которая гнездо свое марает.
It is an ill bird that fouls its own nest. *Cf.* 133

Пуля 683 Не пуля, а человек, из ружья убивает.
[It is not the bullet but the gunman that kills.]
The wise man blames the archer, not the arrow.

684 Пуля найдет виноватого.
Every bullet has its billet. *Cf.* 710

Пушка 685* Из пушки по воробьям не стреляют.
(За мухой с обухом не гнаться/нагоняешься.)
Don't use a cannon to shoot a sparrow.
You can't kill flies with a spear.
Take not a musket to kill a butterfly.

Пьян 686 Пьян об угол не ударится.
Drunken folks seldom take harm.

687 Пьян проспится, а глуп (дурак) - никогда.
A drunk man will sober up, but a damn fool never.

688   Пьяному (и) море по колено (+ а лужа по
ушам).
[The sea is knee-deep for a drunk (+ but a puddle is
up to his ears).]
Whiskey made the rabbit hug the lion.

Пятница   689   Не суйся пятница прежде четверга.
[Friday must not thrust itself before Thursday.]
Don't put the cart before the horse.
Every day is not Friday, there is also Thursday.

Р

Работа

690 (Всякая) работа мастера хвалит.
Work commends the master.
The work shows the workman.

691 Не работа сушит, а забота.
Worry kills more men than work.

692 Не то забота что много работы, а то (забота) как ее нет.
No work is worse than overwork.

693 Работа дураков любит.
[Work loves fools.]
Only fools and horses work.

694* Работа (дело) не волк (медведь) - в лес не убежит (уйдет).
[Work is no wolf (bear) - it won't run away into the woods.]
The best way to get rid of work is to do it.

Работать

695* Кто не работает, тот не ест.
Those who will not work shall not eat.

Радость	696	Радость без печали не бывает.

Радость без печали не бывает.
(Печаль без радости, ни радость без печали не бывает.)
(Где радость, там и горе.)
No pleasure without pain.
No weal without woe. No joy without annoy.
Sadness and gladness succeed each other.   *Cf.* 19, 861

Разговор   697   Разговор дорогу короче делает.
Cheerful (pleasant) company shortens the miles.
Good company on the road is the shortest cut.

698   Разговорами (баснями) сыт не будешь.
Fair words fill not the belly.

Разум   699   Разум силу преодолеет (победит).
Wisdom is better than strength.   *Cf.* 757

Рана   700   Без раны зверя не убьешь.
[You cannot kill the beast without wounding it.]
Omelettes are not made without the breaking of eggs.   *Cf.* 439, 997

Редко   701*   Редко - да метко.
[Rare but apt.]
The best carpenter makes the fewest chips.

Ремесло	702	Худое ремесло лучше хорошего воровства. [An ill-paying job is better than a lucrative heist.] *Better beg than steal.*
Решето	703	Бей в решето когда в сито не пошло. [Use a sieve if it didn't pass through the bolter.] *If at once you don't succeed, try and try again.*
Решить	704	Решено - вершено. Settled once, settled forever. *A decision made cannot be recalled.*
Риск	705*	Риск - благородное дело. [Risk is a noble business.] The more danger, the more honor.
Родиться	706	Что родится, то годится. [Whatever has been born has a purpose.] *There's reason in all things.* **Cf.** 673
Рожа	707	У худой рожи и худой обычай. There is never a foul face but there's a foul fancy.
Рожон	708	Трудно против рожна прати. It is hard to kick against the pricks. **Cf.** 105
Роза	709*	Нет розы без шипов. (Хорош цветок, да остер щипок.) No rose without a thorn.

Рок   710   Рок головы ищет.
[Fate seeks its victim.]
Each cross has its inscription. **Cf.** 684

Рот   711   В закрытый рот муха не залетит.
A closed mouth catches no flies.
Flies fly not into a shut mouth.

     712*   На чужой каравай (пир), рот не разевай (не надейся).
[On another's pie (feast), open not your mouth (do not rely).]
Covet not that which belongs to others.
Thrust not your feet under another man's table.

     713*   На чужой (всякий) рот(ок) не накинешь платок (пуговицы не нашьешь).
[You cannot gag (button) other peoples' mouths.]
People will talk.

     714   Ртом болезнь входит, а беда выходит.
[Through the mouth disease enters and trouble exits.]
The mouth is the executioner and doctor of the body.

     715   У кого во рту желчь, тому все горько.
An ill stomach makes all the meat bitter.

Рубаха	716*	Всякому своя рубаха к телу ближе. (Рубашка к телу ближе.) Near is my shirt, but nearer is my skin. *Every man is nearest himself.* **Cf.** *34*
	717	Рубаха кафтана ближе. Near is my coat but nearer is my shirt.
Рука	718*	Рука руку моет (+ и оба белы бывают). (Левая рука правой помогает.) One hand washes the other.
	719	Своя рука владыка. [Your hand is master.] *Man is his own master.* *A strong man and waterfall channel their own path.*
	720*	Хорошо чужими руками жар загребать. [It's nice to bank up the fire with others' hands.] *It's good to take the chestnuts out of the fire with the cat's (dog's) paw.*
Рыба	721	Большая рыба маленькую целиком глотает. The great fish eat up the small.
	722	Либо (или) рыбку съесть, либо (или) на мель сесть. [Either eat the fish or run aground.] *Either sink or swim. Win or lose.* **Cf.** *607*

723   Лучше маленькая рыбка чем большой таракан.

Better are small fish than an *empty dish* [a big roach].

724*   На безрыбье и рак рыба.

Who cannot catch fish, must catch shrimps. *Cf.* 921

725*   Рыба ищет где глубже, а человек где лучше.

[Fish seek where it's deeper, men where it's better.]

Change of pasture makes fat calves.

726   Рыба мелка, да уха сладка.

[Even small fish make a good soup.]

The greatest crabs be not all the best meat.

727*   Рыба с головы (начинает) портится (тухнет).

Fish begins to stink at the head.

Рыбак   728*   Рыбак рыбака (дурак дурака) (свой свояка) видит из далека.

(Рука руку знает.)

[One fisherman (fool) knows another from afar.]

Scabby donkeys scent each other over nine hills.

It takes one to know one.

Рыболов   729   Рыболова одна тоня кормит.

[Only one haul feeds the fisherman.]

One at a time is good fishing.

С

Сава	730	На волки слава а овец таскает Сава.
		(Там дрова рубят, а к нам щепки летят.)
		[Sava rustles the sheep and the wolves get the blame.
		(They hew the logs and we get the chips.)]
		One does the scathe and another has the scorn.
		One does the harm and another hears the blame.
		One beats the bush and another has the bird. Cf. 922
Сажа	731	Около сажи (огня) (терна) ходить - очернишься (ожжешься) (уколишься).
		He that handles pitch shall be defiled.
		If you play with fire you get burnt.
		He that handles thorns shall prick his fingers. *Cf.* 653
Сани	732*	Люби(шь) кататься, люби и саночки возить.
		[If you like to ride, you must carry the sleigh.]
		They that dance must pay the fiddler. Cf. 493, 526
	733*	Не в свои сани не садись.
		[Do not sit in another's sleigh.]
		Paddle your own canoe.
		The cobbler must stick to his last. Cf. 738

Сапог	734*	Два сапога - пара.
		(Одного поля ягоды.)
		[Two shoes make a pair.
		(Berries of the same field.)]
		As like as two peas.

Сапожник	735*	Сапожник без сапог.
		[The shoemaker without shoes.]
		A shoemaker's son always goes barefoot.

Сват	736	Сват свату холодный друг.
		[Two matchmakers make cool friends.]
		One potter envies another.
		Two of a trade seldom agree.

| Свежий | 737 | Свежее всегда лучше. |
| | | Newer is truer. |

Сверчок	738	Знай сверчок свой шесток.
		[The cricket should know its hearth.]
		The cobbler should stick to his last. **Cf.** 733

| Свет | 739 | Невозможного на свете нет. |
| | | Nothing is impossible. |

	740*	Свет не. без добрых людей.
		[The world is not without good people.]
		It is a good world, if it holds.
		The sun shines on all the world.

741 Свет не клином сошелся.
[The world hasn't shrunk to a wedge.] *i.e.* there's a choice.
The world is a wide parish (place).
There are more ways to the wood than one. Cf.
513

Свинья 742* Посади свинью (дурака) за стол - она (он) и ноги на стол.
[Sit a pig (fool) at the table and he'll put his legs up.]
Give a fool an inch and he'll take a mile (yard) (ell).

743 Свинье не до поросят коли ее палят.
A bletherin' cow soon forgets her calf.

744 Свинья и в золотом ошейнике - все свинья.
(Обезьяна и в золотом наряде обезьяна.)
A pig in the parlor is still a pig.

745 Свинья не знает в апельсинах вкусу.
[A pig cannot judge the flavor of oranges.]
A pig used to dirt turns up its nose at rice boiled in milk.

Семеро 746* Семеро одного не ждут.
[Seven do not wait on one.]
The majority rules.
The absent are always in the wrong.

Семь	747*	Семь бед - один ответ. [Seven crimes, one punishment.] *As well be hanged for a sheep as for a lamb.*
	748*	Семь (десять) раз отмерь (примерь), один раз (однажды) отрежь. Measure *twice* [seven (ten) times], cut once.
Семья	749*	В семье не без урода. (Скандал и в благородном семействе.) Accidents will happen in the best regulated families. *There are black sheep in every flock.*
Сердце	750	Путь к сердце мужчины лежит через (его) желудок. The way to a man's heart is through his stomach.
	751*	Сердцу не прикажешь. (Милому насильно не быть.) Love cannot be compelled.
	752	Что ближе к сердцу, то скорее и на языке. What the heart thinks the tongue speaks.
Сеять	753*	Что посеешь (кто что посеет), то и сожнешь (пожнет). (По семени и плод.) As you sow, so you reap. He that sows good seed, shall reap good corn. *Cf.* 651

754 Сей слезами, радостью пожнешь.
They that sow in tears shall reap in joy.

Сидение 755 Худое сидение лучше хорошего хода.
[Bad sitting is preferable to good walking.]
Don't stand when you can sit (and don't sit when you can lie down). Better rue sit than rue flit.

Сило 756 Где сило, там и закон.
(Сило закон ломит/преступает).
Might makes right.

757 Сило уму уступает.
Wisdom is better than strength.
Policy goes beyond strength. *Cf.* 699

Синица 758* Лучше синица (рябчик) (голубь) в руках (руке) (тарелке)
чем журавль в небе (два на ветке) (глухарь на току).
A bird in the hand is worth two in the bush.
Better a sparrow in the hand than a pigeon on the roof.

Сказать 759* Сказано - сделано.
No sooner said than done.

760* Скоро (сказка) сказывается, да не скоро (дело) делается.
(Говорить легко, делать трудно.)
(Не все всегда творится что просто говорится.)
(От слова не сделается.)
Sooner (easier) said than done.
Nothing happens from saying so.
Saying so don't make it so.

Скобель 761 После скобели топором (не тешут).
[After the adze the axe is not used.]
There's little left for the broom after the besom.

Скоморох 762 Всяк (всякий) спляшет, да не всяк (как) скоморох.
All are not merry that dance lightly.

Скоро 763 Что скоро, то хворо (не споро).
Haste makes waste. *Cf.* 828, 874

Слава 764 Добрая слава дороже богатства.
A good name is better than riches.

765 Добрая слава лежит (за печкой спит), а худая бежит (по свету бежит).
A good reputation stands still, a bad one runs.

Сладкое	766	Сладкое с излишеством сделается горьким.

Сладкое | 766 | Сладкое с излишеством сделается горьким.
[Sweet in excess becomes bitter.]
Too much sweet spoils the best coffee.
Too much pudding will choke a dog. **Cf.** 524

Слеза | 767 | Всякому свои слезы (сопли) солены.
(Всякому своя болячка/рана больна.)
(Больны раны на своих плечах.)
[Everyone's own tears (phlegm) (wounds) are bitter (painful).
(Painful are the wounds on one's own shoulders.)]
It's easy to bear the misfortunes of others.
Everyone can master a grief but he that has it.

768 | Слеза скоро сохнет.
Nothing dries sooner than tears.

769* | Слезами (плачем) горю не поможешь.
[Tears (crying) do (does) not relieve grief.]
Tears bring nobody back from the grave. **Cf.** 514

Слепой | 770 | В царстве слепых, кривой царь (и кривому честь).
(Меж слепых и кривой зрячий.)
In the kingdom of (among) the blind, the one-eyed is king.

771 Слепой слепца водит, оба в яму (ни зги не
видят).
If the blind lead the blind, both shall fall into the
ditch.

Слово 772 Давши слово держись, а не давши крепись.
Be slow to promise and quick to perform. *Cf.* 995

773 Много слов, мало дел.
All talk and no action.
The greatest talkers are the worst doers.

774 От слова до дела далеко (целая верста).
[From word to deed is far (a whole mile).]
Saying and doing are two different things. *Cf.* 561

775* Слово не (что) воробей, вылетит - не
поймаешь.
(Сказавши, слово не воротишь.)
[A word is (not) like a sparrow, you cannot catch it
once it has flown.]
A word spoken is past recalling.
Words have wings and cannot be recalled.

776* Слово серебро - молчание золото.
Speech is silvern, silence golden.

777* Ты ему слово - а он тебе десять.
[For your one word he has ten to answer.]
Spur a jade a question and (s)he'll kick you an
answer.

Случай	778	У случая на затылке нет волосов. Take time (occasion) by the forelock, for she is bald behind.
Слушать	779	Больше слушай, меньше говори. Hear much, speak little.
Слыть	780	Не слыть, а быть. Be what you appear to be.
Смелость	781	Без смелости не возмешь крепости. [Without courage you will not capture the fortress.] *Faint heart never won fair lady.*
Смерть	782*	Двум (семи) смертям не бывать, а одной не миновать. (Раньше смерти не умрешь.) [You cannot die two deaths nor escape one. (You will not die before your death.)] *A man can die but once.*
	783	Лучше смерть нежели позорный живот. Better to die with honor than to live with shame. *Cf.* 30
	784	Не столько смертей сколько скорбей. There are more threatened than stricken. *Cf.* 201
	785	От всего вылечишься, кроме смерти. (От смерти нет лекарства/не отлечишься). There is a remedy for everything but death. *Death defies the doctor.*

786 Смерть не за горами, а за плечами.
[Death is not over the hills but over your shoulder.]
At every hour death is near.
Death keeps no calendar.

787 Смерть терпеть легче нежели ждать.
Fear of death is worse than death itself.

788 Счастливым прежде смерти назваться нельзя.
Praise no man till he is dead.
Call no man happy till he is dead.

789 У смерти все равны.
(Смерть не разбирает чина.)
Death is the great leveler.
Death and the grave make no distinction of persons.

Смеяться 790 Кто скоро смеется, тот скоро и плачет.
(Сегодня в цветах, а завтра в слезах.)
[Who is soon to laugh is soon to cry.
(Flowers today, tears tomorrow.)]
After laughter, tears.
Laugh before breakfast, you'll cry
before supper (sunset).

791* Хорошо смеется тот кто смеется последним.
He laughs best who laughs last.

Смола	792	Смола к дубу не пристанет.

Смола к дубу не пристанет.
[The sap won't stick to the oak.]
Virtue is a thousand shields.
Virtue is the safest helmet.

Снег 793 Первый снег - не зима, первая зазноба - не невеста.
[The first snow does not mean winter, nor the first love marriage.]
Those whom we love first we seldom wed.

Собака 794 Бешена собака и хозяина кусает.
(Злобный пес и господина грызет.)
The mad dog bites his master.

795 Будешь меня любить, так и собаку мою люби (не бей).
Love me, love my dog.

796 Была бы собака, а палка будет (камень найдется).
A staff is quickly found to beat a dog.

797 Всякая собака в доме львом кажется.
(Всякий пес в своей конуре лют.)
Every dog is a lion at home. *Cf.* 418, 615

798 Двум собакам одной кости не поделить.
Two dogs over one bone seldom agree.

799   Живая собака (кляча) лучше мертвого льва (рысака).
(Мертвый лев хуже живой собаке.)
Better a live dog than a dead lion.

800   Кто спит с собаками, встает с блохами.
If you lie down with dogs, you will get up with fleas.

801   Не все собаки кусаются которые лают.
(Собака что лает редко кусает.)
Barking dogs seldom bite. *Cf.* 201, 784

802   Собака и на владыку лает.
A little dog will run a lion out of his own yard.

803*   Собака на сене лежит, сама не ест и другим не дает.
The dog in the manger won't eat the oats nor let anyone else eat them.

804   Собака собаку не съест.
Dog does not eat dog. *Cf.* 135, 109

805   Собаке собачья и смерть.
[A dog dies a dog's death.]
An ill life, an ill death.
Such life, such death.

806   Старая собака не привыкнет ощейника носит.

An old dog won't be easily brought to wear a collar.

807   Старую собаку новым фокусам не научишь.
You cannot teach an old dog new tricks.

808   У всякой собаки своя кличка.
No *stone* [dog] without its name.

Сова   809   Покажется (полюбится) сова (сатана) лучше (пуще) ясного сокола.
[Love makes the owl (devil) seem prettier than a white falcon.]
There are no ugly loves nor handsome prisons.
Love is blind. Cf. 459, 460

Совесть   810   Добрая совесть не боится клевет(ы) (лжи).
A clear conscience fears not false accusations.

811   Совесть паче тысячи свидетелей.
Conscience is a thousand witnesses.

Совет   812   Всякий совет к разуму хорош.
Good counsel never comes amiss.
A word to the wise is sufficient.

813   Кто не слушает советов, тому не чем помочь.
He that will not be counselled, cannot be helped.

814   Совет - хорошо, а дело лучше (а два лучше).
Actions speak louder than words.

Согрешить   815   Чем согрешил, тем и накажешься.
Like fault, like punishment.

Сокол   816   Сокол с места, а ворона на место.
[When the falcon's gone the crow succeeds him.]
Seldom comes a better.
Bad is called good when worse comes along.

Солдат   817   Солдат в отпуску - рубаха из порток.
[A soldier on furlough lets his shirt hang out of his trousers.]
All work and no play makes Jack a dull boy.
A little nonsense now and then is relished by the best of men.

Соловей   818   Пой лучше хорошо щегленком чем дурно соловьем.
[Better sing well among the finches than poorly among the nightingales.]
Better be the head of a dog (fox) (mouse) (lizard) than the tail of a lion.

Солома	819*	Если б(ы) (кабы) знал (знать) где упаду (упасть), так соломки подостлал (подстелил) бы. [If I knew where I'd fall, I would have laid a mat.] *If things were to be done twice, all* *would be wise.*
Соломинка	820*	Утопающий (кто тонет), ухватится и за соломинку (за острый мечь). A drowning man will clutch at a straw.
Солнце	821*	И на солнце бывают пятна. There are spots even in the sun.
Соль	822	Без соли стол кривой. [The table is crooked without salt.] *Salt seasons all things.*
Сон	823	Сон лучше всякого лекарства. Sleep is better than medicine.
	824	Сон смерти брат. Sleep is the brother of death.
Сосед	825	Ближний сосед лучше дальней родни. A near friend is better than a far-dwelling kinsman. Better a neighbor near than a brother far. A friend at hand is better than a relative at a distance.

Сосна	826	Не все сосны в лесу корабельные.
		[Not all pines in the wood are fit for a ship.]
		Every block will not make a Mercury.
Спасибо	827	Из спасибо (поклонов) не шубу шить (шапки не сошьешь).
		(Спасибо в карман не кладут.)
		[You can't make a fur (cap) out of "thanks."]
		You can't put "thanks" into your pocket.
		Thanks is poor pay. Fine words butter no parsnips.
Спешить	828*	Поспешишь - людей насмешишь.
		[Make haste, make laughter.]
		Haste makes waste.
		Haste trips up its own heels. **Cf.** 763, 874
Спор	829	Дале (дальше) в спор, больше слов.
		Wranglers never want words.
Сравнение	830	Все познается в сравнении.
		Nothing is good or bad but by comparison.
Ссора	831	Для ссоры нужны двое.
		It takes two to quarrel.

Старость	832	Под старость человек либо умный, либо глупый бывает. [On the threshold of old age one is either wise or a fool.] *Every man is a fool or a physician at forty.*
	833	Старость не радость. Age brings grief.
	834	Щеголял смолоду, а под старость умирает с голоду. (Смолоду прореха - под старость дыра.) An idle youth, a needy age. *He that corrects not small faults will not control great ones.*
Старуха	835	Живет и на старуху проруха. (И на Машку промашка.) [Even an old lady (Masha) can blunder.] *Even Homer sometimes nods.* *Nobody's perfect.*
Старший	836	Почитай старших, сам будешь стар. Who honors not age is not worthy of it.
Старый	837*	Кто старое помянет, тому глаз вон. [Who brings up the past, out with his eyes.] *Let bygones be bygones.* **Cf.** 74
	838	Чем старее, тем правее. Older and wiser. The older the better.

Стена	839	Белая стена дуракам бумага. A white wall is a fool's paper.
	840	У стен бывают уши. Walls have ears.
Стол	841	Многие за столом храбры. Many are armchair generals. *Cf.* 262
	842	На чужом столе хорош обед. (В чужих руках калач слаще.) [The dinner is good on another man's table.] *The wholesomest meat is at another man's cost.* Another man's *food* [pie] is sweeter.
Сторона	843*	Со стороны виднее. Lookers-on see most of the game.
Страна	844	Всякая страна человеку отечество. A wise man esteems every place to be his own country.
Страх	845	Страх путь кажет. Fear is a great inventor.
	846*	У страха глаза велики. Fear has magnifying eyes.

Судьба	847	Желающего судьба ведет, нежелающего - тащит. Fate leads the willing but drives the stubborn.
	848	От судьбы не уйдешь. No flying from fate.
Сукно	849	Под толстым сукном не хуже согреешься как под бархатом. [A coarse cloth will warm you no worse than velvet.] *As good a broth may come out of a wooden ladle as out of a silver spoon.*
Сума	850	От сумы да от тюрьмы не отказывайся (отрекайся). [Don't dismiss the beggar's cup nor the prison cell.] *No fence against a flail.* *Never say never.*
Сухарь	851	Свои сухари лучше чужих пирогов. (Чужое и хорошее - постыло, а свое и худо - да мило.) Dry bread at home is better than roast meat abroad. *Cf.* 931
Счастливый	852	Счастливому везде добро (хорошо) (счастится). [The lucky man does well everywhere.] *He dances well to whom fortune pipes.*

853   Счастливый и в огне не сгорит и в воде не потонет.
[A lucky person will neither burn in a fire nor drown in the water.]
Give a man fortune (luck) and cast him into the sea.

854   Счастливый ходит, на клад набредет, а несчастный пойдет и гриба не найдет.
[A lucky man will stumble upon a treasure while an unlucky one can't even find a mushroom.]
Some people would fall down a sewer and find a ring.

Счастье   855   Иному счастье - мать, а иному - мачеха.
Fortune to one is mother, to another is stepmother.

856   Легче счастье найти нежели удержать.
'Tis easier to find happiness than to keep it.

857*   Не было (бы) счастья, да несчастье помогло.
[There would be no good fortune had misfortune not helped.]
There's no great loss without some gain.
A blessing in disguise.

858   При счастье приятелей много везде, а прямого друга узнаешь в беде.
In time of prosperity, friends will be plenty, in time of adversity, not one amongst twenty.

859   Счастье лучше богатства.
It is better to be *born* lucky than rich.
Better be fortunate than rich.

860   Счастье многих обманывает.
Fortune is fickle.

861   Счастье с несчастьем двор обо двор живут (об межу живут).
(Счастье и несчастье на одном коне/полозу ездят/едут.)
[Fortune and misfortune ride the same horse (sled).]
Fortune and misfortune are next-door neighbors.
Great fortune brings with it great misfortune. *Cf.* 19, 696, 946

862   Храбрым счастье помогает.
(Смелому Бог помогает.)
Fortune favors the bold.

    863   И малому есть счет.
[Even a small thing has its worth.]
No hair so small but has its shadow.

864   Короткий (ближний) (дале) (чаще) счет - длинная (дальняя) (ближе) (дольше) дружба.
Short reckonings (accounts) make long friends (friendship).

Сытый   865*   Сытый голодного не разумеет.
He whose belly is full believes not him who is fasting.

Т

Теленок	866	Ласковый теленок две матки сосет. [A loving calf is suckled by two mothers.] *Be friendly and you will never want friends.*
Тело	867*	В здоровом (здравом) теле здоровый (здравый) ум (дух). A sound mind in a sound body.
Терпение	868*	Всякому терпению бывает конец. Patience has its limits.
	869	Терпение дает умение. Diligence makes an expert workman. They that have patience may accomplish anything.
	870*	Терпение и труд все перетрут. [Patience and work will overcome all.] *Patience wears out stones.* *Time and patience change the mulberry leaf to satin.*
	871	Терпение - лучшее спасение. Patience is the best remedy for every trouble.

Теснота	872*	В тесноте, да не в обиде. [Tight but all right.] *The more, the merrier.*
Тихо	873	Лучше тихо да вперед, чем скоро да назад. [Better slowly forward than quickly back.] *Speed will get you nowhere if you're going in the wrong direction.* **Cf.**
	874*	Тише едешь, дальше будешь. Slow and steady wins the race. Make haste slowly. *Cf.* 763, 828
Товар	875	Всякому товару цена есть. There is no good that does not cost a price.
	876	Не похваля товар не продашь. (Не хуля, не купишь - не хваля, не продашь.) He praises who wishes to sell. He that blames would buy.
	877	Товар лицом продается. (Хороший товар сам себя хвалит.) Pleasing ware is half sold. Good ware makes quick markets.
Тонко	878*	Где тонко (веревка тонка), там и рвется. The thread breaks where it is weakest. *A chain's only as strong as its weakest link.*

Топор	879	Тонул топор сулил - а вытащили и топорища жаль. Vows made in storms are forgotten in calms. *Cf.* 202
Точность	880	Точность - вежливость королей. Punctuality is the politeness of princes.
Трава	881	После нас хоть трава не расти (хоть потоп). After us, the deluge.
Трезвый	882*	Что у трезвого на уме, то у пьяного на языке. What soberness conceals, drunkenness reveals.
Третий	883*	Третий - лишний. (Где двое, там третьему дела нет). [Third is extra.] Two's company but three's a crowd.
Труд	884*	Без труда не вынешь рыбку из пруда. [You won't get the fish from the stream without work.] *A cat in gloves catches no mice.*
	885	Ленивому и одеться труд. A lazy sheep thinks its wool heavy.

886 После трудов, сладок покой.
[After work, rest is sweet.]
Rest is the sweet sauce of labor.
The sleep of a laboring man is sweet.

Тужить 887 О чем тому (перестань о том) тужить чего (чему) нельзя воротить (пособить).
Never grieve for what you cannot help.
It's no use crying over spilt milk. Cf. 31

Тула 888* В Тулу со своим самоваром не ездят.
[One doesn't bring *samovars* to Tula.]
Carry coals to Newcastle.

Ты 889 Как про тебя сказывали, таков ты и есть.
[As people describe you, so you are.]
If one, two or three tell you you are an ass, put on a bridle.
When all men say you are an ass, it is time to bray.

890 Люблю тебя, да не как себя.
[I love you, but not like myself.]
All men love themselves more than another.
Every man is nearest himself. Cf. 34

891 Ты - мне, я - тебя.
Scratch my back and I'll scratch yours.

У

Уговор	892*	Уговор дороже денег. [An agreement is better than money.] *An honest man's word is as good as his bond.* *Agree, for the law is costly.*
Ужин	893	После ужина (гриппа) горчица. After *meat* (dinner) [the flu] mustard. *Cf.* 441, 448
Ум	894	Без ума житье - рай. [Living mindlessly is paradise.] *Ignorance is bliss.*
	895	Великие умы сходятся. Great minds think alike.
	896*	Живи своим умом. Use your [own] head. *Live your life, don't copy it.*
	897	Задний ум лучше переднего. Hindsight is better than foresight.
	898*	Каждый (всяк) (всякий) по-своему с ума сходит (бесится). (Всяк дурак на свой лад с ума сходит.) [Every man (fool) goes mad in his own way.] Every man is mad on some point.

899   На час ума не стало, навек дураком
прослыыл.
[Lose your head for an hour and be labeled a fool
forever.]
One wrong thought may cause a lifelong regret.
*One foolish mistake can undo a lifetime of
happiness.*

900   Ум без разума беда.
[Knowledge without reason is a calamity.]
There's no fool like a learned fool.

901   Ум пришел, да пора прошла.
[When sense came the time had passed.]
When a fool has made up his mind, the market's
over.

902*   Ум хорошо, а два лучше.
Two *heads* [minds] are better than one.

903*   Чужим умом долго не проживешь (умен не
будешь) (не выстроишь дом).
[You cannot get by long (be smart) (build a house)
with another's wits.]
Every tub must stand on its own bottom.

Умный   904   Умный молчит а дурак ворчит.
Wise men silent, fools talk.

Ус   905   Ус в честь, а борода и у козла есть.
[Whiskers are fine, but even a goat has a beard.]
If the beard were all, the goat might preach.

Услуга   906*   Услуга за услугу.
(За добро добром и платят.)
One good turn deserves another.
Repay kindness with kindness. *Cf.* 257

Уста   907   Устами младенца глаголет истина.
(Мал малышок, а мудрые пути кажет.)
From the mouths of babes springs truth.

Утро   908*   Утро вечера мудренее.
Night brings counsel.

Ухо   909*   В одно ухо вошло (влетает), в другое вышло (вылетает).
In one ear and out the other.

Учение   910   Для учения нет старости.
Never too old to learn.

911   Корень учения горек, а плод сладок.
Knowledge has bitter roots but sweet fruits.
Lessons hard to learn are sweet to know.

912*   Учение свет (атаман) (красота) - а неучение тьма (комар) (сухота).
There is only one good - knowledge, there is only one evil - ignorance.

913   Учение лучше богатства.
Better wit than wealth.
Knowledge is better than riches (wealth).

Учить   914*   Ученого учить - только портить.
(Не учи ученого.)
(Не учи белого лебедя/рыбу/щуку плавать.)
[Teaching only spoils the scholar.
(Do not teach a scholar.)
(Do not teach the white swan/fish/pike to swim.)]
Do not (try to) teach your grandmother to suck eggs.

915   Учить иных - научиться и сам.
To teach another is to learn yourself.

Ф

| Факт | 916 | Факты - упрямая вещь.
Facts are stubborn things. |
| Факт | | |

Факт 916 Факты - упрямая вещь.
Facts are stubborn things.

Фаля 917 Всякая Фаля сама себя хвалит.
Every ass likes to hear himself bray.

Федот 918* Федот, да не тот.
[It's Fedot, but not that Fedot.]
No like is the same.

Филат 919 У каждого Филятки свои ухватки.
[Every Filat has his own trick.]
Every man has his hobby horse.

Философ 920 Философ смерти не боится.
[The philosopher does not fear death.]
The whole life of a philosopher is a preparation for death.

Фома 921 На безлюдье и Фома человек (дворянин).
[When there's no one else, St. Thomas will do (is noble).]
For want of company, welcome trumpery. **Cf.** 724

922   Не наказывай Фому за Еремину вину.
[Don't blame Tom for Jerry's fault.]
Tobiah sinned and Sigud is beaten. **Cf.** *730*

923*   Я ему (говорят) про Фому, а он (мне) про Ерему.
[I'm talking about Tom and he tells me about Jerry.]
He that conceives amiss answers amiss (worse).
Who understands ill, answers ill.

924   Шутить над Фомой (другом), так и любить (шутку) над собой.
(Чему посмеешься/позавидуешь, тому сам поработаешь/того сам берегись.)
If you make a jest [about Thomas], you must take a jest.
To laugh at someone is to be laughed back at.

X

Хата	925*	Моя хата с краю - ничего не знаю. [My house is on the edge, I know nothing.] *What one doesn't know can't hurt him.* *See no evil, hear no evil, speak no evil.*
Хвалить	926	Сам себя ни хвали ни хули. Neither praise nor dispraise thyself.
Хвост	927	Будь без хвоста, да не кажись кургуз(а). [Be a bobtail, but don't look docked.] *Cry not before you are hurt.* *A short-tailed dog wags his tail same as a long one.*
Хлеб	928	Без хлеба не жить, да не от хлеба жить. Man must eat to live but not live to eat.
	929	Едешь на день, бери хлеба на неделю. Who goes for a day into the forest, should take bread for a week.
	930	Кто голоден никогда не скажет что хлеб худ. Hunger never saw bad bread.

931 Лучше есть хлеб с водой чем калач с бедой.
A crust of bread in peace is better than a feast in contention. *Cf.* 851

932 Не давай голодному хлеба резать.
[Don't give a hungry man bread to slice.]
The doghouse is no place to keep a sausage.

933* Не хлебом единою сыт (жив) человек.
Man lives not by bread alone.

934 Около хлеба и мыши водятся.
No larder but has its mice.

935 Хлеб всему голова.
Bread is the staff of life.

936 Хлеб-соль ешь, а правду режь.
[Break bread as you like, but speak the truth accurately.]
Call a spade a spade.
Tell it like it is.
Speak from the shoulder.

Хозяин 937 Всяк хозяин в своем доме (царствует в доме своем).
Every man is a king (master) in his own home.

| | 938 | Где хозяин ходит, там земля родит.
The master's footsteps fatten the soil. |

Хозяйка 939 Хозяйкою дом стоит.
The wife is the key of the house.

Хорошо 940* Все хорошо что хорошо кончается.
All's well that ends well.

941* Там хорошо где нас нет.
(Славны бубны за горами.)
[It's always better wherever we happen not to be.
(The tambourines are fine over the hills.)]
The grass is always greener on the other side of the fence.
Distance lends enchantment.
Distant hills look greener. **Cf.** 359

942* Хорошего понемножку (понемногу).
(Все хорошее не сразу).
You can have too much of a good thing. **Cf.** 366

Хотение 943 Хотение найдет причину.
Where there is a will there is a way.

Храбрый 944 Храброму не нужна длинная шпага,
A brave arm makes a short sword long.

Хрен	945*	Хрен редьки не слаще.
		There's little choice in rotten apples.
Худо	946*	Нет худа без добра.
		(Во всяком худе не без добра.)
		No evil without some good.
		Nothing so bad in which there is not something of good. *Cf.* 19, 861
	947	Худо до добра не доведет.
		Good can never grow out of evil.
	948	Худо нажитое (чужое добро) в прок нейдет.
		Ill-gotten goods never prosper.

Ц

Цветок	949	Хорош цветок, да скоро вянет.

The fairest flowers soonest fade.

950* Это еще (только) цветочки (присказка), а ягодки (сказка) впереди.
(Час от часу не легче.)
[These are but the blossoms (introduction), the berries (fable) are (is) yet to come.]
Cheer up--the worst is yet to come.

Цель 951 Цель оправдает средства.
The end justifies the means.

Церковь 952 Близко церкви да далеко от Бога.
(Около святых черти водятся.)
The nearer the church, the farther from God.
The devil lurks behind the cross. **Cf.** 44

953 Кто не видал церкви, тот и печи молится.
[He who has never seen a church, prays to his hearth.]
Acorns were good until bread was found.
He that never ate flesh thinks pudding a dainty.

954 Не строй церкви, пристрой сироту.
[Don't build a church, provide for an orphan.]
Good deeds are better than creeds.

Цыпленок 955* Цыплят осенью считают.
Don't count your chickens till they hatch.

Ч

Час 956 Не тем час дорог что долог, а тем что
короток.
[An hour is precious not because it is long but
because it is short.]
An inch of time is an inch of gold.

Чека 957 Не велика чекушка, а без нее не уедешь.
[A cotter-pin may be small, but you cannot ride far
without it.]
Great businesses turn on a little pin.
Great engines turn on small pivots.

Человек 958 Человек не без греха.
(На кого грех/ошибка не бывает.)
No man is infallible.
Every man has his besetting sin.

959 Человек не для себя родится.
We are not born for ourselves.

960 Человек предполагает а Бог располагает.
Man proposes, God disposes.

961 Человек человеку волк.
Man is to man a wolf.

962*   Человеку (людям) свойственно ошибаться.
(На грех мастера нет.)
To err is human.

963*   Чтобы узнать человека, надо семь (три) пуд(а)
соли с ним съесть.
(Узнавай человека не год, не два, а семь лет.)
(Вдруг не станешь друг.)
Before making a friend, eat a bushel of salt with
him.
It takes a year to make a friend.

Червь   964   Наступи на червя - извиваться будет.
Tread (step on) a worm and it will turn.

Чердак   965   В   пустой   чердак   двойных   стекол   не
вставляют.
[You don't install double windows in an empty
garret.]
They don't put marble tops on cheap furniture.

Черт   966*   В тихом(их) омуте(ах) черти водятся.
Still waters run deep.

967   Когда черт не сможет чего сделать, посылает
бабу.
When the devil can't go, he sends his grandmother.

968   На чертей только слава.
[Only the devils get fame.]
A bad deed never dies.
Mankind bestows more applause on her destroyer
than on her benefactor.

969*   Не так страшен черт как его малюют.
The devil is not so black as he is painted.   *Cf.* 243

970   Черт своих не берет.
The devil is good (kind) to (protects) his own.

Честь   971   В тайном деле чести нет.
We cannot come to honor under coverlet.

972   По заслугам и честь.
Give credit where credit is due.
We get out of life exactly what we put into it.

973   Трудным путем высокая честь достижается.
The greater the obstacle, the more glory in overcoming it.
No flowery road leads to glory.

974 Честь на волоске висит, а потеряешь так и канатом не привяжешь.
[Honor hangs on a hair, but once it's lost not even a cable will fasten it.]
Glass, china and reputations are easily cracked and never well-mended.

975 Честь переменяет нравы.
Honors change manners.

976 Честь честью, а дело делом.
[Honor is honor, but business is business.]
Honor and profit lie not in one sack.

Чудеса 977* Чудес не бывает.
[Wonders don't exist.]
A wonder lasts but nine days.
Wonder is the daughter of ignorance.

Чуть 978* Чуть-чуть (почти) (один раз) не считается.
A little doesn't count.
Almost is not good enough.

Ш

Шаг	979	От великого до смешного один шаг. From the sublime to the ridiculous is but one step.
Шило	980	Погонишься за шилом, топор потеряешь. [Go aftwer the awl and you'll lose the hatchet.] *Lost with an apple and won with a nut.*
	981*	Шила в мешке не утаишь. [You cannot conceal an awl in a sac.] An eel cannot be hidden in a sac. *The truth will out (come to light) (has no confines).*
Шуба	982	Из ежевой кожи шубы не сошьешь. (Из шерсти шелка не сделаешь.) [You can't make a fur from a hedgehog's hide. (You can't make silk from wool.)] *You cannot make a silk purse out of a sow's ear.*
Шутить	983	Шутить хорошо до краски. Leave a jest when it pleases lest it turn to earnest.

Шутка   984   В каждой шутке есть доля правды.
(В шутках правды бывает.)
Many a true word is spoken in jest.

              985   Шутка, минутка - а заражает на час.
[A joke lasts a minute but it sticks for an hour.]
A laugh a day makes the world seem gay.

Щ

Щеня	986	Щеня злое от злой суки.

Щеня злое от злой суки.
We may not expect a good whelp from an ill dog.
Cf. 426

Я

Яблоко 987 От одного порченого яблока, целый воз загнивает.
One bad (rotten) apple spoils the bunch (its neighbors). *Cf.* 568

988 Яблок на сосне не бывает.
(Не расти на вербе/елке грушу/яблочку.)
[Apples don't grow on pines.]
Ask pears of an elm tree.
One can't gather grapes of thorns or figs of thistles.

989* Яблоко от яблони не далеко падает (откатывается).
(Мимо яблони яблоко не падает.)
The apple never falls far from the tree.

Язык 990* Язык без костей (мягкий), а кости ломает.
The tongue breaks bone and itself has none.

991 Язык мал, великим человеком шатает.
[The tongue is small, but makes a great man tremble.]
Under the tongue men are crushed to death.

992*   Язык мой - враг мой.
       My tongue is my enemy.

993   Язык не стальной, а режет.
       The tongue is not steel yet it cuts.

994*   Языком болтай, а рукам воли не давай.
       [Let you tongue ramble on, but keep your hands
       still.]
       Words may pass but blows fall heavy.   *Cf.* 63, 190

995   Языком не спеши, а делом не ленись (спеши
       делом).
       Be slow to promise and quick to perform.   *Cf.* 772

Яйцо   996   Лучше лишиться яйца чем курицы.
       Better give the *wool* [egg] than the *sheep* [hen].

997   Не разбивши яиц, не сделаешь яичницу.
       You cannot make an omelette without breaking
       eggs.   *Cf.* 439, 700

998*   Яйца курицу не учат.
       Eggs can't teach the hen.

| Яма | 999* | Не рой другому (для друга) яму - сам в нее попадешь (ввалишься).
(Что другу желаешь, то сам себе получаешь.)
Dig a pit for another and fall into it oneself. |
| Ясли | 1000 | Ясли к лошади не ходят.
(Овес за лошадью не ходит).
[The manger (oats) will not go to the horse.]
The tail does not shake the dog.
Roasted ducks dont't fly into your mouth.   ***Cf.*** 179 |

BIBLIOGRAPHY

RUSSIAN PUBLICATIONS

1. Аникин В.П. *Русские народные пословицы, поговорки, загадки и детский фольклор.* Москва, 1957.
2. Ашукин Н.С. и Ашукина М.Г. *Крылатые слова.* Москва, 1960.
3. Бабичев Н.Т. и Боровский Я.М. *Словарь латинских крылатых слов.* Москва: Русский язык, 1986.
4. Богданов А.И. *Сборник пословиц и присловиц Российских.* 1741.
5. Буковская М.В. *et al. Словарь употребительных английских пословиц.* Москва: Русский язык, 1990.
6. Гуревич В.В. и Дозорец Ж.А. *Краткий русско-английский фразеологический словарь.* Москва: Русский язык, 1988.
7. Даль В.И. *Пословицы русского народа.* Москва, 1861-1862.
8. Дубровин М.И. *Английские и русские пословицы и поговорки в иллюстрациях.* Москва: Просвещение, 1993.
9. Жуков В.П. *Словарь русских пословиц и поговорок.* Москва, 1966.
10. _____. *Словарь русских пословиц и поговорок.* 4е изд. испр. и доп. Москва: Русский язык, 1991.
11. Княжевич Д.М. *Полное собрание русских пословиц и поговорок, расположенных по азбучному порядку.* Москва, 1822.
12. Кузьмин С.С и Шадрин Н.Л. *Русско-Английский словарь пословиц и поговорок.* Москва: Руский язык, 1989.
13. Кусловская С.Ф. *Сборник английских пословиц и поговорок.* Минск: Вышэйшая школа, 1987.
14. Мартынова А.Н. и Митрофанова В.В. *Пословицы, поговорки, загадки.* Москва: Современник, 1986.
15. Молоткова А.И. ред. *Фразеологический словарь русского языка.* Москва: Русский язык, 1978
16. Пермяков, Г.Л. *От поговорки до сказки - заметки по общей теории клише.* Москва, 1970.
17. _____. *Паремиологический эксперимент. Материалы для паремиологического минимума.* Москва: Наука, 1971.

18. _____. «О смысловой структуре и соответсующей классификации пословичных изречений.» *Перемиологический Сборник* Москва, 1978, 105-135.

19. _____. transl. Filippov, Y.N. *From Proverb to Folk-Tale. Notes on the General Theory of Cliché.* Moscow: "Nauka" Publishing House, 1979.

20. _____. *Паремиологические исследования. Сборник статей.* Москва: Наука, 1984.

21. _____. *300 общеупотребительных русских пословиц и поговорок (для говорящих на болгарском языке).* Москва: Русский язык, 1986.

22. _____. *Основы структурной паремиологии.* И.Л.Елевич ред. Москва: Наука, 1988.

23. Снегирев И.М. *Русские народные пословицы и притчи.* Москва, 1848.

24. Соболев А.И. *Русские пословицы и поговорки.* Москва, 1983.

25. Тарланов, З.К. «Особенности синтаксиса русских пословиц.» *Русская Речь,* no. 4(1977), 56-59.

26. Фелицина, В.П. «О пословицах и поговорках как материалы для фразеологического словаря.» *Проблемы фразеологии. Исследования и материалы.* Ed. А.М. Бабкина. Москва, 1964. 200-204.

27. _____ и Прохоров Ю.Е. *Русские пословицы, поговорки, и крылатые выражения, Лингвострановедческий словарь.* Москва: Русский язык, 1988.

28. Шейдлин, Б. *Москва в пословицах и поговорках.* Москва, 1929.

BIBLIOGRAPHY

OTHER PUBLICATIONS

1. *(anonymous).* "Russian Proverbs." *The Quarterly Review,* 139 (1875).
2. Altenkirch, R. "Die Beziehungen zwischen Slaven und Griechen in ihren Sprichwörten." *Archiv für slavische Philologie,* 30 (1908-1909), 1-47; 321-364.
3. Aroutunova, Bayara. "Gesture and Word: A Semiotic Treatment of Russian Phraseologic Expressions and Proverbs." *Folia Slavica,* 3, nos. 1-2 (1979), 48-79.
4. Bauer-Czarnomski, F. *Proverbs in Russian and English.* London, 1920.
5. Carey, Claude. *Etude des proverbes russes recueillis et non publiés par Dal' et Simoni.* Diss. Harvard University, 1966. Published under the title *Les proverbes érotiques russes. Etudes de proverbes recueillis et non-publiés par Dal' et Simoni.* The Hague: Mouton, 1972.
6. Disraeli, Isaac. *Curiosities of Literature.* London: Routledge, 1834.
7. Dundes, Alan. ed. *The Study of Folklore.* Englewood Cliffs, 1965.
8. _____. "On the Structure of the Proverb." *Proverbium* 25 (1975), 961-973.
9. Fuller, T. *Gnomologia: Adagies and Proverbs; Wise Sentences and Witty Sayings, Ancient and Modern, Foreign and British.* London, 1732.
10. Georges, Robert A. & Dundes Alan. "Toward a Structural Definition of the Riddle." *Journal of American Folklore.* 76 (1963) 117.
11. Geyr, Heinz. *Sprichwörter und sprichwortnahe bildungen im dreisprachigen Petersburger Lexikon von 1731.* Bern: Peter Lang, 1981.
12. Grzybek, Peter. "Foundations of Semiotic Proverb Study." *Proverbium* 4 (1987) 39-85.
13. _____. "Two Recent Publications in Soviet Structural Paremiology." *Proverbium* 6 (1989) 181-186.
14. Guershoon, Andrew. *Certain Aspects of Russian Proverbs.* Diss. University of London, 1941. London: Frederick Muller, 1941.

15. Hazlitt, W.C. *English Proverbs and Proverbial Phrases.* London: Reever and Turner, 1869.
16. Henderson, A. *Scottish Proverbs.* Edinburgh, 1832.
17. Jaszczun W., Krynski, S. *A Dictionary of Russian Idioms and Colloquialisms.* University of Pittsburgh Press, 1967.
18. Kuznetsova A. *Без пословицы речь не молвится.* Munich, 1964.
19. Levin, Maurice Irwin. *Repetition as a Structural Device in the Russian Proverb.* Diss. Harvard University, 1964.
20. _____. "The Structure of the Russian Proverb." *Studies Presented to Professor Roman Jacobson.* Ed. Charles E. Gribble. Cambridge, Mass.: Slavica Publishers, 1968. 180-187.
21. Mawr, E.B. *Analogous Proverbs in Ten Languages.* London: Elliot Stock, 1885.
22. Mertvago, Peter. *The Comparative Russian-English Dictionary of Russian Proverbs and Sayings.* New York: Hippocrene, 1995.
23. Mieder, Wolfgang. *International Proverb Scholarship: An Annotated Bibliography.* New York: Garland Publishing, 1982.
24. _____. *International Proverb Scholarship: An Annotated Bibliography.* *Supplement I*. New York: Garland Publishing, 1990.
25. _____. "Paremiological Minimum and Cultural Literacy." in *Wise Words: Essays on the Proverb.* ed. W. Mieder. New York: Garland Publishing, 1994.
26. Mieder W., Kingsbury S.A., Harder K.B. *A Dictionary of American Proverbs.* Oxford: Oxford University Press, 1992.
27. Milner G.B. "What is a Proverb?" *New Society* 332 (6 Feb.69), 199-202.
28. _____. "Quadripartite Structures." *Proverbium* 14 (1969), 379-383.
29. Otto, H. *Die Sprichwörter und sprchwörtlichen Redensarten der Römer.* Leipzig, 1890.
30. Permiakov G.L. "О логическом аспекте пословиц и поговорок." *Proverbium* 10 (1968), 225-235.
31. _____. "О лингвистическом аспекте пословиц и поговорок." *Proverbium* 11 (1968), 276-285.
32. _____. "О предметном аспекте пословиц и поговорок." *Proverbium* 12 (1969), 324-328.
33. _____. "On the Paremiological Level and Paremiological Minimum of Language." *Proverbium* 22 (1973), 862-63.

BIBLIOGRAPHY

34. _____. "On Paremiological Homonymy and Synonymy." *Proverbium* 24 (1974), 941-943.

35. _____. "Наиболее употребительных русских сравнительных оборотов типа присловий." *Proverbium* 25 (1975), 974-979.

36. _____. *300 allgemeingebräuchliche russische Sprichwörter und sprichwörtliche Redensarten.* Moskau: Russki jazyk and Leipzig: VEB Verlag Enzyklopädie, 1985.

37. _____. "On the Question of a Russian Paremiological Minimum." English translation K.J. McKenna. *Proverbium* 6 (1989) 91-102.

38. Rothe, Richard. "Russische Sprichwörter." *Sprachpflege*, 11 (1962), 210-11.

39. Rothstein, Robert A. "The Poetics of Proverbs." *Studies Presented to Professor Roman Jacobson.* Ed. Charles E. Gribble. Cambridge, Mass.: Slavica Publishers, 1968. 265-274.

40. Seiler, F. *Deutsche Sprichwörterkunde.* Handbuch des deutschen Unterrichts IV.III. München, 1922.

41. Sigal, Georges. "Dictons et proverbes russes: Reflets d'une psychologie collective toute différente de celle des français." *Revue de psychologie des peuples*, 25 (1970), 308-324.

42. Stevenson, Burton. *The Macmillan (Home) Book of Proverbs, Maxims and Familiar Sayings.* New York: Macmillan, 1948.

43. Strafforello, Gustavo. "Filosofia dei proverbii russi." In G. Strafforello. *Curiosità ed amenità letterarie.* Firenze: L.Niccolai, 1889. 126-132.

44. Taverner, R. *Proverbs or Adagies with newe addicions gathered out of the Chiliades of Erasmus.* London, 1539.

45. Taylor, Archer. *The Proverb.* Hatboro, Pennsylvania, 1962.

46. Whiting, B.J. "Proverbs and Proverbial Sayings: Introduction." *The Franck C. Brown Collection of North Carolina Folklore.* Vol.1. Durham, 1952.

47. Wilson, F.P. *The Oxford Dictionary of English Proverbs.* 3rd ed. Oxford: OUP, 1970.

48. Yermoloff. *Die Landwirtschaftliche Volksweisheit in Sprichwörtern, Redensarten und Wettergeln.* Leipzig, 1905.

Other Russian Interest Titles Available from Hippocrene Books . . .

Dictionaries

RUSSIAN PHRASEBOOK AND DICTIONARY
256 pp • 3,000 entries •
0-7818-0190-7 • $9.95pb • (597)
Cassettes: 0-7818-0192-3 • $12.95 • (432)

RUSSIAN-ENGLISH/ENGLISH-RUSSIAN
STANDARD DICTIONARY, Revised
418 pp • 32,000 entries • 0-7818-0280-6 • $18.95pb • (322)

DICTIONARY OF BUSINESS AND LEGAL TERMS, Bilingual
800 pp • 40,000 entries • 0-7818-0505-8 • $35.00pb • (617)

RUSSIAN-ENGLISH/ENGLISH-RUSSIAN CONCISE DICTIONARY
536 pp • 10,000 entries • 0-7818-0132-X • $11.95pb • (262)

RUSSIAN-ENGLISH/ENGLISH-RUSSIAN COMPACT DICTIONARY
536 pp • 10,000 entries • 0-7818-0537-6 • $9.95pb • (688)

TUTORIAL BEGINNER'S RUSSIAN
200 pp • 0-7818-0232-6 • $9.95pb • (61)

MASTERING RUSSIAN
278 pp • 0-7818-0270-9 • $9.95pb • (11)
Cassettes: 0-7818-0271-7 • $12.95 • (13)

DICTIONARY OF RUSSIAN VERBS
750 pp • 20,000 entries • 0-88254-420-9 • $35.00pb • (10)

Culinary

THE BEST OF RUSSIAN COOKING, Revised edition
270 pp • 0-7818-0131-1 • $9.95pb • (251)

Travel

THE RUSSIAN FAR EAST
311 pp • 0-7818-0325-X • $18.95pb • (114)

LANGUAGE AND TRAVEL GUIDE TO RUSSIA
219 pp • 0-7818-0047-1 • $14.95pb • (321)

Literature

TREASURY OF RUSSIAN LOVE POEMS
128 pp • 0-7818-0298-9 • $11.95hc • (591)
Cassettes: 0-7818-0364-0 • $12.95 • (586)

TREASURY OF CLASSIC RUSSIAN LOVE SHORT STORIES, Bilingual
128 pp • 0-7818-0601-1 • $11.95 • (674)

DICTIONARY OF RUSSIAN PROVERBS, Bilingual
477 pp • 5,335 entries • 0-7818-0424-8 • $35.00pb • (555)

DICTIONARY OF PROVERBS AND THEIR ORIGINS
by Linda and Roger Flavell
250 pp • 5 ½ x 8 ½ • 0-7818-0591-0 • $14.95pb • (701)

TREASURY OF LOVE PROVERBS FROM MANY LANDS
146 pp • 6 x 9 • illus • 0-7818-0563-5 • $17.50hc • (698)

INTERNATIONAL DICTIONARY OF PROVERBS
580 pp • 5 ½ • x 8 ½ • 0-7818-0531-7 • $29.50hc • (656)

COMPREHENSIVE BILINGUAL DICTIONARY OF FRENCH PROVERBS
400 pp • 5 ½ x 8 ½ • 6,000 entries • 0-7818-0594-5 • $24.95pb • (700)

DICTIONARY OF 1,000 FRENCH PROVERBS
131 pp • 5 x 7 • 0-7818-0400-0 • $11.95pb • (146)

DICTIONARY OF 1,000 GERMAN PROVERBS
131 pp • 5 ½ x 8 ½ • 0-7818-0471-X • $11.95pb • (540)

DICTIONARY OF 1,000 ITALIAN PROVERBS
131 pp • 5 ½ • x 8 ½ • 0-7818-0458-2 • W • $11.95pb • (370)

DICTIONARY OF 1,000 JEWISH PROVERBS
David C. Gross
Jewish proverbs, ancient and contemporary, encompass a wide range of subjects, reflecting lives that were often impoverished materially but rich spiritually. These old and new proverbs became part of the Jewish people's heritage and were not only passed on through the generations, but also expanded upon continually.

The one thousand proverbs offered here are arranged by Hebrew subject, followed by a transliteration into English from either Hebrew, Yiddish, or Aramaic followed then by an English translation. For easy reference, a complete English index of the subjects appears at the back of the book.
131 pp 5 ½ x 8 ½ • 0-7818-0529-5 • W • $11.95pb • (628)

DICTIONARY OF 1,000 POLISH PROVERBS
131 pp • 5 ½ x 8 ½ • 0-7818-0482-5 • $11.95pb • (628)

A TREASURY OF POLISH APHORISMS, A Bilingual Edition
Compiled and translated by Jacek Galazka
Twenty years ago *Unkempt Thoughts*, a collection of Polish aphorisms by
Stanislaw Jerzy Lec was published in English and became an instant success.
Clifton Fadiman called Lec: "one of the remarkable wits of our dark time,
eminently attuned to it." A selection of his aphorisms opens this collection, which
comprises 225 aphorisms by eighty Polish writers, many of them well known in
their native land. A selection of thirty Polish proverbs is included representing
some uniquely Polish expressions of universal wisdom. These were translated by
Helen Stankiewicz Zand, a noted translator of Polish fiction. Twenty pen and ink
drawings by a talented Polish illustrator Barbara Swidzinska complete this
remarkable exploration of true Polish wit and wisdom.
140 pp • 5 ½ x 8 ½ • 20 illustrations • 0-7818-0549-X • $12.95 • (647)

**COMPREHENSIVE BILINGUAL DICTIONARY OF RUSSIAN
PROVERBS**
edited by Peter Mertvago
477 pp • 8 ½ x 11 • 5,335 entries, index • 0-7818-0424-8 • $35.00pb • (555)

DICTIONARY OF 1,000 SPANISH PROVERBS
131 pp • 5 ½ x 8½ • bilingual • 0-7818-0412-4 • $11.95pb • (254)

A CLASSIFIED COLLECTION OF TAMIL PROVERBS
edited by Rev. Herman Jensen
499 pp • 3,644 entries • 0-7818-0592-9 • 19.95pb • (699)

Slavic Interest Titles Available from Hippocrene Books . . .

Dictionaries

ENGLISH-AZERBAIJANI/AZERBAIJANI-ENGLISH
CONCISE DICTIONARY
144 pp • 5 x 7 • 8,000 entries • 0-7818-0244-X • $14.95pb • (96)

BYELORUSSIAN-ENGLISH/ENGLISH-BYELORUSSIAN
CONCISE DICTIONARY
290 pp • 4 x 6 • 6,500 entries • 0-87052-114-4 • $9.95pb • (395)

CHECHEN-ENGLISH/ENGLISH-CHECHEN
DICTIONARY AND PHRASEBOOK
160 pp • 3 x 7 • 1,400 entries • 0-7818-0446-9 • $11.95pb • (183)

ESTONIAN-ENGLISH/ENGLISH-ESTONIAN
CONCISE DICTIONARY
300 pp • 4 x 6 • 6,500 entries • 0-87052-081-4 • $11.95pb • (379)

GEORGIAN-ENGLISH/ENGLISH-GEORGIAN
CONCISE DICTIONARY
346 pp • 4 x 6 • 8,000 entries • 0-87052-121-7 • $8.95pb • (392)

GEORGIAN-ENGLISH/ENGLISH-GEORGIAN
DICTIONARY AND PHRASEBOOK
150 pp • 3 x 7 • 1,300 entries • 0-7818-0542-2 • $11.95pb • (630)

LATVIAN-ENGLISH/ENGLISH-LATVIAN
PRACTICAL DICTIONARY
474 pp • 4 ⅜ x 7 • 16,000 entries • 0-7818-0059-5 • $16.95pb • (194)

LITHUANIAN-ENGLISH/ENGLISH LITHUANIAN
CONCISE DICTIONARY
382 pp • 4 x 6 • 10,000 entries • 0-7818-0151-6 • $14.95pb • (489)

LITHUANIAN-ENGLISH/ENGLISH LITHUANIAN
COMPACT DICTIONARY
400 pp • 3 x 4 • 10,000 entries • 0-7818-0536-8 • $8.95pb • (624)

RUSSIAN-ENGLISH COMPREHENSIVE DICTIONARY
Oleg Benyukh, General Editor
Containing over 40,000 entries and 100,000 references, this is the most thorough, accurate and up-to-date Russian-English dictionary in the world. It also includes phonetic transcriptions, parts of speech, appropriate idiomatic usage, and appendices of common given names, geographical locations, weights and measures, Latin words and phrases and tables of numbers and temperature. It has been described as the ultimate reference tool for students, scholars and business people.
800 pp • 6 x 9 • 0-7818-0506-6 • $60.00hc • (612)

ENGLISH-RUSSIAN COMPREHENSIVE DICTIONARY
800 pp • 8 • x 11 • 50,000 entries • 0-7818-0353-5 • $60.00hc • (312)
0-7818-0442-6 • $35.00pb • (50)

RUSSIAN-ENGLISH/ENGLISH-RUSSIAN STANDARD DICTIONARY
Revised Edition with Business Terms
418 pp • 5 x 8 • • 32,000 entries • 0-7818-0280-6 • $18.95pb • (322)

ENGLISH-RUSSIAN STANDARD DICTIONARY
214 pp • 5 • x 8 • 16,000 entries • 0-87052-100-4 • $11.95pb • (239)

RUSSIAN-ENGLISH/ENGLISH-RUSSIAN CONCISE DICTIONARY
536 pp • 4 x 6 • 10,000 entries • 0-7818-0132-X • $11.95pb (262)

RUSSIAN-ENGLISH/ENGLISH-RUSSIAN COMPACT DICTIONARY
536 pp • 3 1/8 x 4 5/8 10,000 entries 0-7818-0537-6 • $9.95pb • (688)

RUSSIAN HANDY DICTIONARY
120 pp • 5 x 7 • 0-7818-0013-7 • $8.95pb • (371)

RUSSIAN PHRASEBOOK AND DICTIONARY, Revised
256 pp • 5 x 8 • 3,000 entries, subway maps of Moscow and St. Petersburg
0-7818-0190-7 • $9.95pb • (597)
2 cassettes: 120 minutes • 0-7818-0192-3 • $12.95 • (432)

RUSSIAN-ENGLISH/ENGLISH-RUSSIAN DICTIONARY OF BUSINESS AND LEGAL TERMS
800 pp • 5 x 8 • 40,000 entries • 0-7818-0163-X • $50.00 • (617)
0-7818-0505-8 • (480) $35.00pb

DICTIONARY OF RUSSIAN VERBS
Includes 20,000 fully declined verbs.
750 pp • 5 x 8 • • 0-7818-0371-3 • $45.00 • (572)
0-88254-420-9 • NA • $35.00pb • (10)

TATAR-ENGLISH/ENGLISH-TATAR CONCISE DICTIONARY
400 pp • 4 x 6 • 8,000 entries • 0-7818-0250-4 • $11.95pb • (278)

UKRAINIAN-ENGLISH/ENGLISH-UKRAINIAN STANDARD DICTIONARY
590 pp • 5½ x 8 ½ • 32,000 entries • 0-7818-0374-8 • $24.95pb • (193)

UKRAINIAN-ENGLISH STANDARD DICTIONARY
286 pp • 5 ½ x 8 ½ • 16,000 entries • 0-7818-0189-3 • $14.95pb • (6)

UKRAINIAN-ENGLISH/ENGLISH-UKRAINIAN PRACTICAL DICTIONARY
Revised Edition with Menu Terms
406 pp • 4 • x 7 • 16,000 entries • 0-7818-0306-3 • $14.95pb • (343)

UKRAINIAN PHRASEBOOK AND DICTIONARY
205 pp • 5 ½ x 8 ½ • 3,000 dictionary entries • 0-7818-0188-5 • $11.95pb • (28)
2 cassettes: 120 minutes • 0-7818-0191-5 • $12.95 • (42)

UKRAINIAN-ENGLISH/ENGLISH-UKRAINIAN COMPACT DICTIONARY
448 pp • 3 x 4 • 8,000 entries • 0-7818-0498-1 • $8.95pb • (610)

UZBEK-ENGLISH/ENGLISH-UZBEK CONCISE DICTIONARY
329 pp • 4 x 6 • 7,500 entries • 0-7818-0165-6 • $11.95pb • (4)

Tutorial

BEGINNER'S RUSSIAN
200 pp • 5 ½ x 8 ½ • 0-7818-0232-6 • $9.95pb • (61)

MASTERING RUSSIAN
278 pp • 5 ½ x 8 ½ • 0-7818-0270-9 • $14.95pb • (11)
2 Cassettes: • 0-7818-0271-7 • $12.95 • (13)

BEGINNER'S UKRAINIAN
130 pp • 5 ½ x 8 ½ • 0-7818-0443-4 • $11.95pb • (88)

RUSSIAN FABLES, BILINGUAL EDITION
Ivan Krylov
Translated by Bernard Pares

"Once in the froggies favour, Democracy had lost its savour ...."
Thus begins a classic fable about the consequences of vain wishes,
"The Frogs ask for a King," in which the frogs petition Jupiter for a
ruler. The god answers with first a poplar log, to which the bored
frogs heartily object, and second a stork, who gobbles up its
unsuspecting subjects. The froggies learn their lesson at a bitter
cost. Jupiter's response to their continuing complaints: "Well, learn
to live with him, or look for even worse!"

Russian fabulist Ivan Krylov was born in Moscow in 1798. His
fables are considered unique because of his use of long iambic
lines and the colloquial inflections, idioms and sayings of the
peasant language. A collection to be enjoyed and treasured, this
beautiful gift volume contains the fables in Russian with
side-by-side English translations as well as handsome llustrations
throughout.

96 pp • illustrations • 6 x 9 • 0-7818-0575-9 • $19.95hc

Travel

THE RUSSIAN FAR EAST
Erik and Allegra Harris Azulay
This guidebook highlights the striking natural beauty of the nine regions which make up the Russian Far East, including active volcanoes, untouched forests, hot springs, and salmon runs, as well as the urban areas and business centers developing in the region. Information is provided on accommodations, restaurants, and transportation by train, car, bus and plane.
311 pp • 6 x 8 • maps, photos • 0-7818-0325-X • $18.95pb • (114)

LANGUAGE AND TRAVEL GUIDE TO RUSSIA
219 pp • 5 • x 8 • 0-7818-0047-1 • $14.95pb • (321)

LANGUAGE AND TRAVEL GUIDE TO UKRAINE
266 pp • 3 x 4 • 4 maps, b/w pictures throughout, index
0-7818-0135-4 • (35) • $16.95pb

THE BEST OF RUSSIAN COOKING, Revised edition
Alexandra Kropotkin
"Russia has a decided culinary heritage. This book reflects that heritage better than any volume I know." —Craig Claiborne
Now updated with a complete list of menu terms, this comprehensive Russian cookbook is better than ever. Three hundred easy-to-follow recipes for popular dishes like Beef Stroganoff and *borscht*, as well as many lesser-known dishes which are daily fare in Russia: *kotleti* (ground beef), *piroshki* (dumplings with meat or vegetables), and *tvorojniki* (cottage cheese cakes).
270 pp • 5 • x 8 • 0-7818-0131-1 • $9.95pb • (251)

THE BEST OF UKRAINIAN CUISINE
Bohdan Zahny
Everything from tantalizing appetizers through desserts and beverages, including such Ukrainian specialties as *zakusky* (appetizers), *ioushky* (cabbage soup), *kasha* (buckwheat groats), pyrishky (stuffed pastries), and medovyky (honey cakes).
295 pp • 5 x 8 • 0-7818-0494-9 • $12.95pb • (304)